HISTORIC KNARESBOROUGH

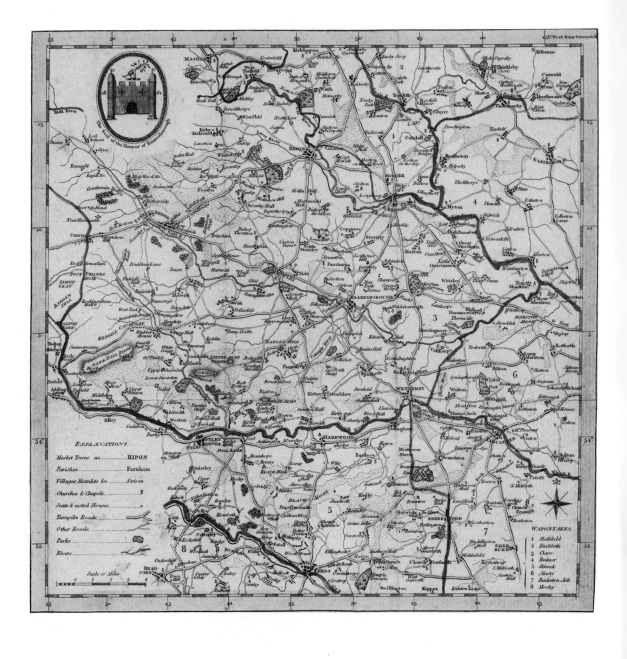

Historic Knaresborough

Arnold Kellett

First published in 1991 by

Smith Settle Limited
Ilkley Road
Otley
LS21 3JP

ISBN Paper 1 870071 59 X
Cloth 1 870071 66 2

Frontispiece:
Map engraved for Hargrove in 1775

Designed, printed and bound by
SMITH SETTLE
Ilkley Road, Otley, West Yorkshire LS21 3JP

Photographic Acknowledgements

The author gratefully acknowledges the following who have given permission for the use of prints, postcards or photographs:
Ackrill Newspapers Ltd, Harrogate, p18, 45, 48, 56, 63, 65, 69, 98(*r*), 101, 102; Miss Elsie Baines, p9(*b*); Miss Joan Barton, p68; Sid Bradley, p20(*tr*); Mrs F Broadbelt, p88; Sir Arthur Collins, p70, 72, 101; Mary Evans Picture Library, p22; Mr John Forster, headmaster, King James's School, p34, 92, 103, 104(*l*); Mr Joseph Fountain, p86, 93; Sqn Ldr David Haller, p96; Mrs Isabel Garbutt, p23, 78, 8(*r*), 84, 90; Harrogate Museums and Art Gallery Services, p52(*r*), 73, 79; Harrogate Resort Services, p27, 105; Peter Kearney, p10, 31; Knaresborough Town Council, p42, 107(*t*); Leeds Central Library, p28, 43; Leeds University Library, p58; Mrs Mary Mann, p14, 39, 83(*l*), 91, 94; Methodist Church (Home Missions), p47; National Railway Museum, p87; North Yorkshire County Archives, p3(*r*), 95; North Yorkshire County Library, p5, 13, 54, 60(*l*), 59, 67, 89; Oldest Chemist's Shop, Knaresborough, p48, 49(*l*); Powell Eddison Freeman and Wilks, p34, 104(*l*); Public Record Office, p11; Mrs M E Pullan, p77; Rayson Gallery, Harrogate, p86; Mr H P Townrow, p71(*l*); Vollans Photography, Knaresborough, p17, 32(*r*), 37, 82; Walton & Co Ltd, Harrogate, p60(*r*), 61, 83(*r*); Weidenfeld and Nicholson Ltd, p9(*l*), 10; Miss E A Willis, p106; Woodmansterne Ltd, p20(*l*); Yorkshire Museum, York, p2; *Yorkshire Post*, p100.

Photographs taken specifically for this book by Richard Littlewood: front cover, p6, 12(*b*), 25, 32(*l*), 33, 49, 52(*l*), 71, 73, 104, 109(*b*).

Photographs by the author: p3(*t*), 4, 9(*tr*), 97, 108.

The rest of the material is from the author's own collection.

FOREWORD

Historic Knaresborough . . . This must surely be the right title for Dr Kellett's latest book about our town. For no town of its size in the North of England has more to offer in the way of history, scenery or beauty. A parish church dating from around 1100, a market with a charter granted in 1310, the oldest chemist's shop in England, started at least in 1720, and the ruins of a medieval castle which dates back to Norman times – these alone show how much there is to cherish. A walk along the Nidd from the World's End and High Bridge gives one views of Tenter Lodge, the parish church, Manor Cottage, the railway viaduct, Castle Bank, the Long Walk and the Dropping Well – each full of history.

In addition, over the years the town has produced many and varied historical personalities: Sir Henry Slingsby, beheaded for his Royalist support in 1658; Blind Jack of Knaresborough, a man of many trades and at the same time an accomplished road surveyor; 'Noisy Tom' Collins, one of Knaresborough's last MPs (for from 1553 Knaresborough returned two members to Westminster); and many others. The story of our castle, Forest, market, King James's School and other institutions gives a fascinating picture of the life and growth of the English town from medieval times to the present.

Who better to tell the story than Dr Arnold Kellett, twice Mayor of Knaresborough? He for many years has diligently studied all aspects of the history of the town, and has recently done detailed research on the origins of the Royal Maundy here, as well as a definitive biography of Eugene Aram, the schoolmaster murderer. His eminently readable text is based on scholarly research, and he has spared no pains to present a factual story based on firm historical facts, lavishly illustrated by authentic prints and photographs.

Why should I write this foreword? I will only say that my family have lived in Knaresborough since the early 1600s. Throughout they have been connected with the parish church, the schools and the welfare of the town. The Rev Thomas Collins was vicar for no less than fifty-three years, 1735–88. Tom Collins was, as I have shown, one of Knaresborough's MPs, and my mother, Lady Evelyn, was Chairman of the Urban District Council in the 1930s. I have been proud to live in Knaresborough all my life, and I feel it vital that for the history of this country, and, indeed, of all our erstwhile dominions and colonies whose laws and customs so closely follow ours, the history of this ancient town shall faithfully be recorded.

Sir Arthur Collins, KCVO, ERD

INTRODUCTION

Knaresborough is above all things historic. Anyone who doubts it will, I trust, be convinced by the evidence I have presented in the following pages. Some of it may come as a surprise, for the facts of the town's connection with Becket's murderers, King John, Richard II, Queen Philippa, the first English spa, royal linen and so forth are not widely known, even amongst residents. The fact is that Knaresborough has a link with so many major national events that its story serves as an introduction to the history of England – and it has so many curious incidents and colourful characters of its own that I am faced with an *embarras de richesses*. In the tricky task of compressing as much of this as possible into a single book, I have had to exclude many favourite items and details of contemporary institutions such as the Bed Race, already part of the town's history.

Knaresborough is not only historic, it is unusually picturesque, offering a wealth of material to engravers, lithographers, painters and photographers. Here is something of the best of what they have recorded over the centuries. For thirty-five years I have been speaking and writing about the history of Knaresborough. But I am the first to concede that one picture is worth a thousand words.

So, first of all, this is a book to browse through, allowing these pictures from the past to speak for themselves. On the other hand, this is not merely a 'picture-book' and I hope you will also carefully read the text, which is a straightforward account of the history of the town, providing in a chronological order the context essential for a real appreciation of the pictures.

As the emphasis in *Historic Knaresborough* is on what can be seen, the text is of necessity comparatively brief – and for further details I would recommend my revised *The Knaresborough Story* (1991), as well as

other books in the bibliography. Better still, in this age of telly-gawping troglodytes and passive armchair history, there is nothing like exploring Knaresborough for yourself. To take just one example, the Parish Church of St John's can provide you with hours of historical interest – the real thing, at first hand. Yet I wonder how many readers have ever made a point of looking round it.

Our ancient parish church has been lovingly restored and conserved. This must be our aim with all that survives of the old buildings, streets and unspoilt scenery of Knaresborough. Through the town council, the civic society and the historical society, supported by the constant vigilance of members of the public, much can be done to preserve the very special character of the town. When I served as a councillor – not as a politician, but as an Independent with a concern for conservation – I was sometimes accused of 'living in the past'. But a sensitive appreciation of the past is a wonderful way of enhancing the present, and I offer this book as a means to that end.

Finally, I must record my gratitude to those who have helped me to produce *Historic Knaresborough*. As there is no comprehensive collection of visual material, I have spent months going round begging and borrowing from various libraries, archives and museums, and especially from Knaresborough folk who have so willingly released their treasured items to add to my own stock of pictures. A few of these have already appeared in my *Knaresborough in Old Picture Postcards,* but some have never been seen by the public before, including rare prints and photographs – *and I must emphasise that all these pictures are strictly copyright.*

I am particularly grateful to Sir Arthur Collins for providing a foreword, and thus setting a kind of hallmark on the book. He is a member of

Knaresborough's most distinguished surviving family, and it has been a privilege to know him, as well as his mother, Lady Evelyn, and other personalities no longer with us, ranging from the venerable Mr W P Lawrence of the Oldest Chemist's Shop, to Lord Inman, who used to wash bottles there as a boy. But such notable Knaresborians would be the first to agree with me that the strength of Knaresborough's past lies not so much in the great and famous as in the multitudes of ordinary people who have no memorial. It is as a tribute to these – the unsung heroes and unrecorded saints no less than the men and women of renown – that *Historic Knaresborough* has been written.

To understand at a glance why Knaresborough came into being, why it has always been admired for its distinctive, dramatic setting and why it is so richly endowed with romantic history, you must stand by the ruined castle and delight in the view. No painting or photograph can begin to do it justice. You have to see it for yourself.

Even on a dull day the panorama is arresting, with the River Nidd some 120 feet below – the far side clothed in magnificent woodland, reminding us that there began the medieval Forest of Knaresborough, and the near side with old houses rising above the river in tiers and terraces, clinging to the rocky gorge. Come here some bright spring morning or sunny summer evening – or, best of all, when the trees are rich with autumn colours and the river is glittering in gentle sunlight – and you will find this scene one of the finest in the world.

Four hundred years ago the poet Michael Drayton enthusiastically described 'the nimble Nyde':

Through Nyderdale along, as neatly she doth glide
Tow'rds Knarsburg on her way . . .
. . . where that brave Forest stands,
Entitled by the Town, who with upprearèd hands
Makes signs to her of joy, and doth with garlands crown
The River passing by . . .

The poet would still find something joyous in the view from the castle. Over the years I have shown it to hundreds of visitors, most of whom have been lost in admiration, because they have never seen anything quite like it – not even in the valley of the Rhine, with which it has often been compared.

The earliest inhabitants, however, were not interested in scenery but in security, and this was certainly provided by such an easily-defended vantage point. There can be little doubt that Knaresborough owes its existence to this area of towering rock, on or near which the first prehistoric encampment must have been made. We are justified in thinking this not only because flint arrowheads, axes and implements have been unearthed in the district, but also because further up the river at Scotton Banks is the site of a prehistoric fort known as Gates Hill, measuring about 380 feet by 200 feet, built on a similar precipitous height above the Nidd.

These first settlers were eventually followed from about 500 BC by the Celts or Ancient Britons. The fiercest of these, the Brigantes, were especially strong in this area, and fragments of their Celtic language survive in local names, such as that of the Nidd itself, and in the traditional method of counting sheep once used in the countryside round Knaresborough.

Hargrove, writing in 1809, maintained that there could still be traced the outlines of a fortified settlement built here by the Ancient Britons, consisting of earth ramparts and ditches. He also believed that the Romans had taken over this fortified area, because several coins of the reigns of Claudius and Constantine had been found in Knaresborough.

All we know for certain is that in AD 74 the Brigantes were finally defeated by the Romans, who built in the midst of conquered Brigantia a walled city of nearly sixty acres called Isurium Brigantum. As this was no further away than the village of Aldborough, six miles to the north-east, we can assume that the Romans knew Knaresborough well, and perhaps had some kind of outpost here. In support of this there is a Roman vase unearthed in Tentergate and a large find of vessels and tools known as 'the Knaresborough hoard', discovered in 1864 by workmen draining farmland between Knaresborough and Aldborough.

Roman pots and pans – part of 'the Knaresborough hoard' on display in the Yorkshire Museum. The bronze bowl on the left is nearly twenty inches in diameter.

The farmer brought a whole cartload to the Knaresborough foundry of Thomas Gott, the ironmonger. Unfortunately many of them were accidentally melted down by an ignorant foreman, but the rest can be seen on display in the Yorkshire Museum, York. There are several tools, including a smith's hammer and carpenter's axes, and a collection of remarkably well-preserved bronze domestic vessels.

Whatever Roman presence there was in Knaresborough, the occupying legions finally returned to Italy in AD 410, leaving Britain wide open to waves of invaders and immigrants from northern Germany – in this part of the country mainly the Angles, the early English, who arrived in about AD 500. We know they had a fortified settlement here, because that is the meaning of the second part of the name Knaresborough – *burgh* in the original Anglo-Saxon. Of at least four explanations of the first part of the town's name, only two are serious contenders. One is that it is the name of some Anglian chieftain, so that it means, for example, 'Cenheard's fortress'. The other is that it preserves the old word *knar* – with the 'k' pronounced – which was used to describe a rough outcrop of rock, an ideal description of the craggy promontory above the Nidd. Comparison with certain other place-names inclines me to this view, and I think Knaresborough could simply be 'the fortress on the rock'.

Soon after the Angles had settled here as farmers, hunters and foresters, they were themselves to suffer from the incursions of other raiders and settlers – Danes, better known as the Vikings, and Norwegians, better known as the Norsemen. From the ninth century these Scandinavians were firmly established, their culture and language mingling with that of the early English. Several street-names originate from that time. Briggate, for example, means 'the street leading to the bridge', Finkle Street is derived from a word for

Part of the ancient Knaresborough Cross, now in St Peter's Church, East Marton.

A Viking-style comb found during the excavation of the castle by Stephen Barber (1925–8).

'angle' or 'corner', and Castle Ings from a word for 'meadow'.

The top of Briggate becomes Gracious Street – a name which seems to suit the churches situated there. But Hargrove is probably correct in deriving this name from Anglo-Saxon *gracht-huys,* 'the houses on the ditch', ie the defensive moat – later an offensive open sewer! The name Kirkgate, 'the street leading to the church', shows that the pagan Knaresborians had been converted to Christianity at an early date – perhaps soon after Gregory the Great sent missionaries to Britain at the end of the sixth century.

There are two interesting confirmations of Christianity amongst the early inhabitants. One is the mention by Saint Bede of a synod held in 705 'near the River Nidd'. The other is part of an ancient stone cross, Christian, but showing a pagan Scandinavian influence. It is described by Pevsner as 'a brilliant piece, with human beings and monsters enmeshed in a wild, tentacle-like interlace'. To see the Knaresborough Cross – one of the earliest evidences of Christianity in the whole of the Harrogate district – it is worth making a journey to St Peter's Church, East Marton, where it was taken by the Roundell family in the eighteenth century.

Another interesting artefact from this period is a comb found during excavations of the castle area in 1925–8 by Stephen Barber. Other relics are in the form of customs. There was, for example, Hoketide, involving a playful stealing of shoes and hats at Easter, which survived in Knaresborough until the middle of the nineteenth century. So did the Knaresborough Sword Dance and the tradition of blessing the plough and pulling it round the town, recently revived each January on Plough Sunday by the Claro Sword and Morris Men.

The Angles and Scandinavians had settled down and coalesced to form a stable early-English community, but it was not long before they were overrun by

The Claro Sword and Morris Men on Plough Sunday. The 'lock' of swords may be a pre-Christian sun symbol. After the traditional sword dance, the plough is pulled through the town.

French-speaking Normans. Following his triumph at Hastings in 1066, William the Conqueror rewarded the knights who had fought with him by granting them territorial units known as manors. One of these was the Manor of Knaresborough, granted to our first known Norman overlord, Serlo de Burgh, a baron from Tonsburgh in Normandy. It seems likely that it was he who started the first stone castle here, and that the Normans used Knaresborough as one of their bases in the ruthless suppression of Northern resistance, the horrific campaign of systematic destruction and massacre known as the Harrying of

the North. By 1070 it is recorded that not a single village remained inhabited between York and Durham.

Knaresborough itself did not escape the devastation, as we see from the Domesday survey of 1086. Here we find recorded the Manor of Chenardesburg with its ten 'berewicks'(villages), including Scriven and Farnham and even far-away Fewston. The manor has 'land for twenty-four ploughs', we read. 'Now it is the King's land, and is waste. In King Edward's time the value was six pounds; it now pays twenty shillings'.

There is no mention of an existing castle in the *Domesday Book*, though by then it would at least be taking shape. Serlo de Burgh had been succeeded as lord of the manor by his brother, the one-eyed John Monoculus, who was married to Magdalen, an aunt of King Stephen. Their son, Eustace Fitz-John, took over the lordship of Knaresborough in 1130, and it is during this year that we find the first known documentary reference to the castle, when the pipe rolls record that Eustace spent '£11 on the King's works at Chenardesburg'.

The king referred to is Henry I, youngest son of William the Conqueror. In addition to developing the castle he seems to have encouraged work on the other fundamental building in the town, the parish church. Indeed, the first documentary reference to the church is earlier than that to the castle. In 1114, the Coucher Book of Nostell Priory, near Wakefield, recorded that the king had given to this Augustinian priory he had recently founded 'the Church of Cnaresburgh with its tythes and chapels'. Whereas practically nothing of the earliest Norman work can be seen in the castle, the church retains foundations and a certain amount of masonry from at least the early twelfth century.

Built like the castle from local magnesian limestone, the church was small and sturdy, extending from the present tower to the east end, where the walls still have the original thickness of four feet. Here we can still

The castle ruins on the precipitous height above the river, as they
appeared in 1805.

A section of the Norman string-course, originally decorating all
the exterior of the church.

trace the outlines of two of the three original windows, and see other examples of Norman architecture in the typical chevron design of the string-course, especially in the vestry, where there is also a Norman window (north) moved here when the vestry was added in the thirteenth century. Ornamentation was less important in those days than strength, and the church – the most substantial building in Knaresborough next to the castle – was built partly as a place of refuge, with the tower to provide a lookout point and to hang a bell. This summoned the people to worship, but was also sounded as a warning. The Norman *couvre-feu*, or curfew, was traditionally rung in Knaresborough every night at eight o'clock from around the time of William the Conqueror until the mid-nineteenth century. If the church had been built, as in many towns, close to the castle, it would have been better protected from the later raids by the Scots, but perhaps the Normans used this sheltered site just above the river because it was already hallowed Christian ground, as the pre-Norman name of Kirkgate suggests.

Records of this period are sparse, but one small item noted in Burton's *Monasticon* shows that the community was beginning to prosper. Cistercian monks had left St Mary's in York to build their own abbey at Fountains in 1132. A year later they were starving, reduced to living on wild herbs, and in their distress turned to Knaresborough for help. Lord Eustace Fitz-John sent them 'a cart-load of fine bread', a gift without which Fountains Abbey might never have been built.

When Fitz-John was killed in battle (in Wales) in 1157, the lordship of Knaresborough went to Hugh de

Morville – the first of the notorious characters to colour the town's history. He was the leader of the four knights who took Henry II at his word when he let slip the unguarded remark: 'Will nobody rid me of this turbulent priest!?' On the 29th December 1170, having murdered Thomas Becket, Archbishop of Canterbury, in his own cathedral, the four assassins fled north to the safety of Knaresborough Castle. According to the Latin chronicle of John de Brompton, these four – de Morville, Richard le Breton, William de Tracy and Reginald Fitz-Urse – were detested by the inhabitants of Knaresborough:

> Everyone used to shun their company, nor would anyone eat or drink with them. They used to eat and drink on their own, and when they threw scraps of food to the dogs, they tasted it, but would not eat it. Behold how the vengeance of God was made manifest: they who had brought contempt on Christ the Lord were despised by the very dogs!

This is not a likely story, but it is vivid historical evidence of the general sense of outrage at the murder in the cathedral. Though the four had powerful friends in the North and were apparently unmolested during the year they are thought to have spent in Knaresborough, they may well have come as penitents to the church before making a pilgrimage to Rome and Jerusalem. Hugh de Morville is said to have made a local act of penance by building Hampsthwaite Church, dedicated to Saint Thomas Becket, who was canonised in 1172.

De Morville had done considerable building in Knaresborough itself, having been authorised by Henry II to strengthen the castle in 1162 at a cost of £90, which represents a significant expenditure. Knaresborough was obviously seen by the Norman kings as a place of strategic value, with the castle ideally situated to help to control the North. Moreover, to the west and south-west of the town was a great tract of largely uncultivated land sufficiently wooded to provide good cover for deer, boar, wild cattle, game-birds – and wolves. First mentioned in 1167, this was known as the Forest of Knaresborough, a royal hunting-ground extending as far as the Washburn Valley, twenty miles from east to west. It consisted of about 100,000 acres – not entirely forest, but with many clearings and settlements, and a scattered population occupied in farming, fishing, charcoal-burning and iron-smelting.

The original Norman manor, known as the Honour of Knaresborough, consisted of three main sections: the Forest of Knaresborough, the Borough or town itself (which actually stood outside the Forest) and the Forest Liberty, comprising a dozen villages on the comparatively level farmland to the north. As each of these three areas was separately administered, with its own court and constables, documentary sources are often of great complexity. In addition, the lesser constables must be distinguished from the Constable of the Castle, the most important official, one of whose duties was to inspect the boundaries of the Forest every three years. This was within the division of the shire known as the wapentake (a Scandinavian term) of Claro (a Norman word).

In 1173 the lordship of Knaresborough passed to William de Stuteville, a relation of de Morville. His son Robert died before reaching his majority, so the boy's uncle, Nicholas de Stuteville, took over as lord. This did not escape the notice of King John, who immediately seized the opportunity to acquire the Honour of Knaresborough for himself. On the pretext that he was not a direct descendant of Robert de Stuteville, the king ordered Nicholas to pay a fine of 10,000 marks – a colossal sum he could not possibly afford. As a result he had to surrender the castle and Forest to the king on the 21st December 1204.

King John now had not only a military stronghold for controlling opposition by the northern barons, but also a base for his favourite sport of stag-hunting. His first move was to appoint as Constable of the Castle an experienced soldier and most able administrator, Brian de Lisle, who came here in 1205 on a stipend which was eventually increased to £48 13s 4d a year. Then John authorised him to strengthen and enlarge the castle, so that it occupied roughly the area we see today. By 1212 Brian de Lisle had spent £1,290 on this work, much of it on the digging out of the enormous dry moat. This extended the natural cliff-like base of the castle – originally all the way round – providing the king with an almost unassailable fortress.

Within a few years Knaresborough Castle had been transformed into what Professor J C Holt, the foremost authority on King John, has described as 'one of the chief military and financial centres of the north'. In addition to the work of rebuilding, the castle was turned into a munitions centre, helping to supply quarrels (crossbow bolts) to the infant royal navy being developed by King John. Made from iron smelted in the Forest of Knaresborough, these quarrels were sent to ports such as Portsmouth and Poole at a rate of 30,000 a year. In 1212 the total manufactured reached 62,000 at a cost of £46 4s 8d. An interesting confirmation of these documentary records was the discovery during Barber's excavations of fifteen small forges in the castle.

For a monarch who was constantly on the move, personally overseeing the administration of his kingdom, King John spent a relatively large amount of time in Knaresborough, visiting it more than any other Yorkshire town except York and Pontefract. There are at least seven recorded visits, the first in 1206. He usually spent one or two nights here – five in 1210 – and on certain occasions he was accompanied by Queen Isabelle, who spent a week here in 1213, when we can assume that she was accompanied by the two princes, Henry aged six and Richard aged four.

As well as inspecting the work on the castle and dealing with administrative matters, King John seems to have found time to relax in Knaresborough. The records show that he lived here in style, with ample food and drink – three barrels of wine on one occasion, and a later order to Brian de Lisle to store no less than twenty tuns of wine (ie 5,040 wine gallons) in the castle. Most important of all, King John went stag-hunting in Knaresborough Forest. The records do not tell us how much venison he brought back, but in 1206 the king paid for 42 palfreys, 11 beagles, 6 other dogs and 3 huntsmen. In 1210 he used huntsmen and 16 dogs, and in 1211 there was payment for 'the care of 22 dogs, one limehound, one dog-keeper and his man, and 9 greyhounds, for eleven weeks by order of the King'.

In spite of King John's reputation as the most ruthless of the Plantagenets – illustrated by the way he treated Nicolas de Stuteville – I have always felt that Knaresborough must have regarded him as a benefactor. In 1972 the Historical Pageant I presented at the castle included a surprisingly benign King John distributing clothing to the poor during Holy Week in 1210. When I was invited as mayor to attend the Royal Maundy in Ripon in 1985, my letter of acceptance mentioned King John's gifts to Knaresborough paupers on the Maundy Thursday of 1210. The Royal Almonry expressed great surprise and interest. According to their records the first known Royal Maundy had taken place at Rochester in 1213.

This naturally plunged me into further research, the result of which is that Knaresborough has now been included in the history books as the place where the first known Royal Maundy was held. The evidence is in King John's personal account of expenses – a rare document and the oldest of its kind – known as the *Rotulus Misae*. Here we read, translating the Latin and allowing for gaps in the text, this entry for the 15th April 1210:

King John and Queen Isabelle played by Dr Richard Rastall and his wife, Jane, in the author's reconstruction of the Royal Maundy of 1210 presented on Maundy Thursday the 16th April 1987.

King John stag-hunting, from an early fourteenth century manuscript. The setting could well be the Forest of Knaresborough, and the dogs exactly fit the documentary references to his hunting here.

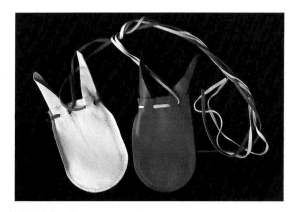

Traditional leather purses of Maundy Money, the red purse containing money 'in lieu of clothing'. These were presented to Harry Butterfield at the Royal Maundy in Ripon Cathedral, 1985.

King John, from his tomb in Worcester Cathedral.

– would have raised their status, as would the knives presented by the king, presumably made in the castle forges.

It was also fascinating to discover that on the following day King John commemorated Good Friday by feeding 100 more paupers in Knaresborough at a cost of 9s 4½d, and paying for the feeding of 1,000 others – probably throughout Yorkshire. Such unprecedented generosity may be explained by the fact that King John was in conflict with Pope Innocent III, who in 1208 had imposed an interdict – a ban on all church services – because of John's refusal to accept Stephen Langton as Archbishop of Canterbury. In November 1209 – only five months before the Knaresborough visit – the Pope, exasperated by King John's continuing obstinacy, had excommunicated him. So it seems that in Knaresborough the king made a point of demonstrating that he was still a loyal son of the Church, a Christian monarch who had every right to associate himself with the tradition of Maundy, humbling himself in Christ-like fashion by giving alms to the poor.

Whether King John's real motive was to impress the Pope, or to demonstrate to the rebellious barons that in spite of the excommunication he was still the rightful monarch, or whether it was simply an act of genuine piety, the occasion was certainly historic. This came across very clearly in the reconstruction we presented in 1987, when it was a moving sight to see the thirteen paupers, played by boys representing all the Knaresborough schools, receive their new clothes from King John. Though clothing is no longer given at the Royal Maundy, the recipients are presented with a red purse containing what is officially described as 'an allowance for clothing and provisions normally given in kind'. It cannot be proved that this unique royal tradition started in Knaresborough, but it is the first such presentation of which there is any record.

King John showed pious generosity to the poor

On the Day of the Lord's Supper in Knaresborough in Maundy [gifts] from the King to 13 paupers, [13 pence each totalling] 14 shillings 1 penny. For the robes of these paupers . . . and for these robes to be sewn: 2 shillings, 2 pence. For 13 belts, 13 knives, 13 pairs of drawers given to these same paupers, and for 13 [pairs of shoes – totalling] 4 shillings 4½ pence [paid by the Abbot] of Bindon.

The Abbot of Bindon was the Royal Almoner. The drawers – underpants, not normally worn by the poor

Part of the *Rotulus Misae* of 1210, recording King John's expenses
in Knaresborough on the first known Royal Maundy.

elsewhere in the country, and here in Knaresborough there were two other indications that he took himself seriously as a Christian monarch. The first was that in 1205 he appointed one of his clerks, Alexander de Dorset, as Vicar of Knaresborough, thus ignoring the rights of Nostell Priory. Alexander, no doubt encouraged by the king, started to enlarge the church in the beautiful style of architecture known as Early English, eventually extending the nave to its present approximate length and height, and creating two chapels or chantries. Alexander de Dorset lived to see the oversight of the church transferred to the Archbishop of York in 1230, when an area surrounding it was created the Prebend of Beechill, an

estate bringing in revenue to the prebendary, who held two courts a year.

The other indication of King John's religious interest was the pilgrimage he made to the hermitage of Saint Robert. Born in York around 1160, Robert Floure (or Flower) had eventually settled as a hermit in the riverside cave near Grimbald Bridge. Though he was never canonised, he came to be known as Saint Robert, famed for his ascetic life, independent spirit and compassion for the poor and prisoners. Legends tell of temptation by demons, miracles of healing and power over wild animals, such as the three stags Robert is said to have harnessed to his plough. He seems to have farmed land near the cave, especially

The castle grounds, showing part of the keep, completed in 1312.

St Robert's Cave as seen by Samuel Howell in 1836. The artist has
exaggerated the height of the rocky platform containing the tomb
recess and the size of the cave entrance.
To the left is Plumpton Mill.

when some was given to him by William de Stuteville, who had been terrified by a demonic nightmare after having threatened to drive Robert from Knaresborough Forest.

King John visited the cave on the 17th February 1216, the year following his signing of the *Magna Carta*. He was accompanied by a small retinue, including Brian de Lisle. When they arrived, Robert, who had the custom of reciting all 150 Psalms every day, was deep in prayer, and refused to get up from his knees. When Brian de Lisle finally persuaded him, Robert asked which one was the king, then held out some ears of corn, asking John, if he was a king, could he create something like that – out of nothing? Embarrassed, the royal entourage said to King John: 'This man is not haille of brayne' (sound of mind). John, however, replied that Robert was the wisest of them all, for he acknowledged only the Almighty. Far from being annoyed, he granted him a carucate of land – as much as he could till with a plough. King John was certainly half as good as his word, because there is documentary confirmation of his gift of forty acres (half a carucate) along the river. Only eight months later King John died, and though the chronicler Matthew Paris claimed that hell would now be even fouler because of his presence, he remained pious to the last, buried at his request in a monk's cowl between two saints in Worcester Cathedral.

After Saint Robert's death, on the 24th September 1218, he became the centre of a cult which brought pilgrims to Knaresborough from far and wide. Armed guards from the castle were sent to prevent monks from Fountains Abbey from taking his corpse. Healing oil is said to have flowed from his tomb, and miracles of healing were attributed to the waters of St Robert's Well. A more substantial sequel to his death was the continuing of his work by the Trinitarian friars of St Robert's Priory.

The first known charter of Knaresborough Priory was granted in 1257 by King John's youngest son, Richard Plantagenet, Earl of Cornwall and Lord of Knaresborough, who gave the friars the land his father had given to Saint Robert. It was on part of this that the priory was built, along one of the loveliest stretches of the river, roughly between the house known as the Abbey and the one known as the Priory, the latter with a few medieval fragments built into the garden wall and the gable-end of an outbuilding. There are also the Aspin ponds, one nearby and one up on the crag top, where the friars (no pun intended) kept their fish.

Sculptured stone from the priory. Why a medieval lion? Because the priory used the arms of its patron, Richard Plantagenet.

The priory gatehouse, situated between the crag
and the River Nidd.

Though almost nothing of the priory has survived, and though only an old print of the gatehouse and a window in Pannal Church gives any idea of its appearance, it was nevertheless of considerable importance, being the only branch of the Trinitarians in Yorkshire. These friars, in their white robes, marked by a cross consisting of a red upright with a blue crossbar, went round begging alms – first for the priory, secondly for the poor and thirdly for use as ransom money to liberate hostages captured during the Crusades. It is said the Trinitarian Order for the Redemption of Captives in the Holy Land – to give them their full title – liberated about 100,000 Christian prisoners, and in Knaresborough they effectively maintained the tradition of Saint Robert until 1538, when they were suppressed by Henry VIII.

Richard Plantagenet was succeeded as Lord of Knaresborough by his son Edmund, who died in 1300 without issue, leaving the Honour to revert to the Crown. While Edward I was alive, all was well in Knaresborough, and it may have been this great castle-maker himself who planned the complete rebuilding of the castle. However, he died in 1307, and his son, Edward II, immediately recalled from exile his favourite, Piers Gaveston, the detested Gascon who had been banished by Edward I because of his corrupting influence on the young prince. He then created him Earl of Cornwall, which meant he now also possessed Knaresborough.

Unpopular though Gaveston was, it must be conceded that, because he was in such good standing with the new king, the status of Knaresborough was raised in two ways. First, the castle was rebuilt on a grand scale. William de Vaux was appointed Constable, Hugh of Titchmarsh, who had worked on the building of Caernarvon Castle for Edward I, was appointed master mason, and there were at least 100 workmen and 11 quarrymen, taking the stone from the quarry near what was later called Staynbrigg

(stonebridge), then March Bridge (from the word for boundary) and finally Low Bridge. When the castle was completed in March 1312, at a cost of £2,174, it must have been a magnificent sight, with its twelve towers and a great keep.

Even today, when it stands as a rough and battered ruin, we can imagine something of its former splendour. The most complete survivals are the twin towers of the barbican gate, in which we can still see the grooves where the portcullis moved up and down, the southern sally-port, the Old Courthouse, with the upper part added at the end of the sixteenth century, and the keep, which stands there like the defiant stump of an old tooth, jagged against the sky. Underneath the keep is the best-preserved part of the whole castle – the dungeon, exactly as it was in the time of Edward II.

With its central column and twelve radiating arches supporting the massive keep, the dungeon is architecturally unique. The tiny window and walls fifteen feet thick ensured there was no escape. We can still see how prisoners were manacled to the wall, and the graffiti they made – especially the one of a stag being killed by an arrow. This is scratched into the stonework near the great, heavy door, where it let in just a chink of light, and we can imagine some poor devil standing there to while away the interminable hours with this primitive art.

The second way in which Knaresborough's status was raised in Gaveston's time was the provision of a charter by Edward II in 1310. Ratified in York the following year, it granted to Gaveston and his heirs not only the Honour, but also the deer parks of La Haye (Haya Park), Bilton and Haverah. The most important part was the declaration:

That Knaresborough be a Free Burgh, and that the men inhabiting the same be Free Burgesses. They shall have one Market and one Fair, with the assize of bread and ale.

16

The dungeon, unchanged since the reign of
Edward II, with its unique arches radiating
from a central pillar, and walls fifteen feet
thick.

An example of medieval graffiti from the castle dungeon: a stag's
head, with a large arrow, bottom left. A prisoner's contemporary
pictorial record of the Forest of Knaresborough.

The last phrase refers to the right to fix a price for staple food and drink. The market, first mentioned in a document of 1206, had probably been held on Wednesday since that time, but the charter officially fixed this as market day, and required all markets and fairs to be announced by the bellman or town crier.

The burgesses, owners of the eighty-six burgage houses, were free townsfolk, to be distinguished from the serfs, villeins or peasants in bondage to a lord and master, who lived mostly outside the town beyond the point still known as Bond End.

Knaresborough now had a new royal castle and its first known charter, but the corrupt Gaveston's unpopularity soon brought about his downfall. The barons, incensed by his conduct under the king's protection, insisted that he should be banished. He was, but was soon recalled from exile once again, and the rebellious barons, led by the king's cousin, Thomas of Lancaster, obliged Edward II to take refuge in Knaresborough Castle in January 1312. The following May they besieged Gaveston in Scarborough Castle, and later the Lord of Knaresborough came to an ignominious end when he was beheaded near Warwick and his head sent to the king.

The troubled reign of Edward II continued with the war against Scotland. Having decided to march north to raise the Siege of Stirling, he found that Lancaster and the barons refused to support him. From York he issued orders to all men between 16 and 60, including those in the Knaresborough district, to join his army. On the 24th June 1314 they faced Robert the Bruce and his victorious Scots in the Battle of Bannockburn, where many Knaresborough men lost their lives, including the Constable of the Castle, William de Vaux.

The opposition led by the king's cousin continued, and on the 5th October 1317 one of the rebels, John de Lilleburn, successfully attacked and occupied Knaresborough Castle. He held it until the 29th January 1318, when it was recaptured by the king's forces led by the new Constable, Roger Damory, who spent £55 on equipment, including a siege-engine, with which he managed to make an eighty foot breach in the curtain wall.

Only a few months later Knaresborough was assaulted by marauding Scots, encouraged by their victory at Bannockburn to make deep incursions into Northern England. Apparently deciding that the castle was too strong to take, they vented their wrath on the town itself. Though they had spared Northallerton and Ripon – the latter paying them 1,000 marks – they set fire to Knaresborough and destroyed 140 out of the 160 houses, as well as burning down the parish church.

The devastation was so serious that Edward II agreed to excuse Knaresborough its customary rents, and the town did not recover until the reign of Edward III and his gracious young queen, Philippa of Hainault. They were married in York Minster in January 1328, when Philippa was only fifteen. Though they appear to have had a week's honeymoon in Knaresborough Castle, it was not until 1332 that Philippa first took up residence here, and this for the excellent reason that the previous year, when she was eighteen, the king had granted her as part of her marriage settlement 'the Castle, Town, Forest and Honour of Knaresborough of the value of £533 6s 8d'.

Queen Philippa lived in style, but she took her responsibilities seriously, in particular restoring the parish church, which was reconsecrated in 1343, originating the local tradition of calling it 'the Queen's Church'. This restoration is seen in the reticulated east window (an exact copy of the original, which survives in the garden of 4 the Avenue), the canopied niches of the west end and especially in St Edmund's Chapel, with its ornamental piscina (basin), sedilia (seat) and Easter sepulchre, all good examples of Decorated architecture.

Queen Philippa, wife of Edward III, had links with Knaresborough from 1328 until her death in 1369. This effigy is from her tomb in Westminster Abbey.

'Queen Philippa's Chest', from the castle.

The town still possesses a sturdy trunk with carrying-handles known as 'Queen Philippa's Chest'. Though the queen was not permanently resident in the castle, she spent a considerable time here with her young family, and her husband when his state duties permitted. Edward III, like King John before him, took an interest in local administration – including visiting St Robert's Priory – and also enjoyed hunting in Knaresborough Forest. During one such hunt in 1355 his life is said to have been saved by Thomas Ingilby of Ripley Castle, who killed the wounded boar that was about to attack him and who was knighted as a reward. The queen seems to have been deeply attached to Edward, on Maundy Thursday 1333 riding all the way from Knaresborough to Durham Priory to see him. She had retired to bed with him, when the monks came to protest that St Cuthbert would not have tolerated the presence of a woman – so Philippa had to leave in her night-clothes and lodge in Durham Castle.

Stories like this must have circulated in medieval Knaresborough, and we can presume a general respect for the queen, who according to Froissart, was tall, beautiful and graceful, 'adorned with every virtue, beloved of God and men'. She spoke her native Flemish, as well as the French still in use amongst the nobility, and had great independence of spirit. She is said to have ridden with the army at the Battle of Neville's Cross in 1346, and a year later was celebrated for the way she pleaded with her husband to spare the six burghers who surrendered the key of Calais. Less well known is her intervention to save the lives of the carpenters at York, when the royal stand they had made for a tournament collapsed.

The one dark episode of Queen Philippa's connection with Knaresborough began in July 1349, when the Black Death struck the town. Since this pneumonic form of bubonic plague spread with such virulent rapidity, wiping out a third of the population of England, we can assume a fearful mortality in the Honour of Knaresborough. Records refer mostly to tenants, whose deaths had to be noted for legal reasons, such as the sixty who had died by October 1349, including the Vicar of Knaresborough, Robert de Neville. The unrecorded death toll amongst the poorest people must have been far greater, and was to be repeated by fresh outbreaks of the plague in 1361 and 1369.

In spite of the Black Death, the resilient local communities gradually returned to normal life, with the courts of the Honour as busy as ever. A few years ago I was handed a document by a private collector which turned out to be a record of proceedings taken in 1356 against William Slingsby and Henry de Scriven, who were accused of extorting sixpence a day from the tenants of Queen Philippa. In addition to parochial matters, Knaresborough also had an interest in national events, such as the exploits of two of Philippa's sons, the Black Prince and John of Gaunt.

John of Gaunt, so called because he had been born to Philippa in 1340 in the Belgian town of Ghent, was to become the new Lord of Knaresborough. Having married the beautiful Blanche of Lancaster (who died of the plague and was lamented in a poem by Chaucer), he inherited her estates and was created Duke of Lancaster in 1362. Queen Philippa died in 1369, and on the 24th June 1372 the widowed Edward III granted to their youngest son, John of Gaunt, the Honour of Knaresborough.

This was a historic date, the beginning of Knaresborough's link with the Duchy of Lancaster, which makes the castle still part of the royal estates. When he became Lord of the Honour, John was thirty-two and married to his second wife, Constance of Castille (who is said to have fled to the safety of the castle during the poll tax rebellion of Wat Tyler). When Constance died in 1394, John of Gaunt married Catherine Swynford, whose sister, a maid of honour to Queen Philippa, had married Geoffrey Chaucer. This justifies the thought that the famous poet may have visited Knaresborough, and the assumption that his son was the Thomas Chaucer, later Speaker of the Commons, who was appointed Constable of the Castle.

Like his father before him, the Duke of Lancaster followed the royal tradition of hunting in the Forest of Knaresborough – as is indicated by the nickname of a ruined hunting lodge in Haverah Park, John of Gaunt's Castle. He does not seem to have spent much time in Knaresborough, however, as he was the richest landowner in the country, with the enormous income of £12,000 a year, and had many other estates and also political intrigues to occupy his time.

John of Gaunt was not a conspicuous success either as a soldier or statesman, and his chief effect on the course of history was through his son, Henry Bolingbroke, who deposed his cousin, Richard II, and was crowned in his place as Henry IV. On John of Gaunt's death in 1399 his estates had been seized by King Richard, and this led the new Duke of Lancaster,

Richard II, the castle's most illustrious prisoner (1399).

now popular and powerful, to demand not only his rightful inheritance, but the king's abdication. Richard was arrested, and because he still had support he was moved around from castle to castle, eventually to Pickering and from there to Knaresborough Castle.

He was here for only a short time – perhaps only one night – but it is easy to imagine his thoughts as he languished, not in the dungeon, but in the King's Chamber in the keep. Here was the anointed King of England, a prisoner in one of his own castles – and one that had been the home of his grandparents (for Richard was the son of the Black Prince). Though Shakespeare in his great tragedy *Richard II* exaggerates Gaunt's patriotism, he wonderfully brings out the pathos of Richard's predicament:

> For God's sake let us sit upon the ground,
> And tell sad stories of the death of kings . . .
> I live with bread like you, feel want, taste grief,
> Need friends: subjected thus,
> How can you say to me, I am a king?

Such melancholy thoughts must have assailed Richard in Knaresborough before he was transferred to Pontefract Castle, where (according to Holinshed) he was murdered by Sir Piers of Exton, who – exactly like Hugh de Morville – had acted in response to an incautious remark made by another King Henry. An alternative tradition is that the heart-broken Richard simply pined to death in prison.

The beginning of the fifteenth century was marked by the construction of the Chapel of our Our Lady of the Crag, carved out of the rockface near Low Bridge by John the Mason in about 1408. Believed to be the third oldest wayside shrine in Britain, this tiny chapel (12 feet by 8 and 7 feet high) is well known because of the mysterious figure guarding the entrance – possibly one of the Knights Templar, who had a base at Little Ribston. The earliest engravings all show the face almost worn away, and the one we now see appears to

The Chapel of Our Lady of the Crag, constructed in 1408, showing the medieval soldier and an Edwardian visitor.

be a nineteenth century concrete replacement. Early guide books refer to this as 'St Robert's Chapel', but it dates from almost two centuries after the saint's death and must simply have been confused with the cave. A little-known poem by Wordsworth shows that he came to see the chapel (probably in 1802). It includes the lines:

I once beheld a Templar Knight . . .
Employed in setting his sword free
From its dull sheath – stern sentinel
Intent to guard Saint Robert's cell . . .

Though wars at this time were mainly confined to Wales and France – including Henry V's famous victory at Agincourt in 1415 – society was far from stable. There was, in fact, a kind of local war being waged between the men of Knaresborough Forest and the Archbishop of York, whose officers attempted to collect taxes on their goods in local markets. In 1439 about 700 foresters terrorised Otley at the July fair, and in 1441 the archbishop had to make Ripon 'like a towne of warre' to keep out the foresters.

Law enforcement was exercised by the constables and the courts for the Forest and Liberty – held in what we know as the Old Courthouse in the castle – and the Borough Court in the tollbooth in the market place. Near here stood the stocks, a later example of which can be seen in the Courthouse Museum. From 1446 there are also references to Knaresborough waits – originally watchmen and later instrumentalists. Then there was the Borough Bailiff, who presided over the fortnightly Borough Court and served as a kind of justice of the peace, as well as market inspector.

There were many examples of lawless behaviour, even from the vicars. The Rev John Browne, for example, was accused in 1435 of breaking down railings in Haya Park with the intention of poaching. He was involved in at least one other court case, and it is not surprising that his name turns up in the scandal surrounding Sir William Plumpton, Master Forester and High Sheriff of Yorkshire, and Joan Wintringham, with whom he lived at Plumpton Hall just outside Knaresborough, and also in Wintringham Hall which once stood at the top of High Street. Summoned before an ecclesiastical court because of his 'unlawful intimacy' with Joan, Sir William produced as witness the parish clerk, who deposed that in 1451 he had been present at a secret wedding performed in the parish church before sunrise by the Reverend John Browne. Having married the couple, the priest said mass 'in a low voice'.

This secret marriage was found to be lawful – an important decision for Sir William, because it established that the son of his clandestine union, Robert, was the rightful heir. This was essential, as a son by Sir William's first marriage had been killed during the Wars of the Roses at the bloody Battle of Towton in 1461 – one of a reported total of 38,000 dead, whose slaughter turned the nearby beck red with blood. The Plumptons and many Knaresborough men were on the losing Lancastrian side, and this turbulent period was to continue until 1485 when Henry Tudor defeated Richard III. The following year, as Henry VII, he married Elizabeth of York, thus uniting her family with the House of Lancaster.

The peaceful symbol of the new Tudor rose can be seen carved in the stonework of the nave in the parish church, which was restored and partly rebuilt during the second half of the fifteenth century in the Perpendicular style. Aisles were added, absorbing the earlier transepts, and there were new windows and buttresses. When the high Transitional roof was lowered at the same time, the tower would have seemed too tall for anything more than the dwarf spire or 'Hertfordshire spike' which was added around 1520, giving the church an attractive and distinctive finish.

The octagonal Tudor font is of particular interest, because we can still see where the original font cover was locked into position to prevent people from stealing the holy water of baptism, in those days permanently kept in the font. The ponderous but intricately-carved cover is a later replacement (dated from the cupid as late Jacobean, around 1685) and suspended from a magnificent wrought-iron bracket of the same date.

Here we have evidence of the fact that Knaresborough once believed in witches – who might attempt to steal water for magical rites. There is an interesting example of this in the case of John Steward, a Knaresborough schoolmaster, who was prosecuted in 1510 for his part in a conspiracy to seek buried treasure by divination. Evidence was given that he had three bumble bees as familiars, which he fed one by one with 'a drope of blode of his fyngor'. Confirmation of the need to lock up the water is the evidence that he was also alleged to have baptised a cock and other creatures.

John Steward was a real person, but Knaresborough's famous witch and prophetess, Mother Shipton, is largely a figure of folklore – with at least one professor of history of the opinion that she never existed. The first reference to her appears in a pamphlet of 1641, which makes no mention of Knaresborough or the date of her birth. It does, however, associate her with York, where she was apparently living in 1530 when Cardinal Wolsey was on a journey there. Mother Shipton is said in the pamphlet to have predicted that he would never reach the city, and it is historical fact that Wolsey, having got as far as Cawood Castle, within sight of York Minster, was arrested on a charge of high treason, taken south – and died on the way in Leicester Abbey.

As this prophecy was printed more than a century after the event had taken place, it is impossible to establish whether it really was made. However, the same pamphlet does describe a future devastation of

St John's Parish Church in its spacious green setting, a haven of peace in the heart of the town.

The entrance to St John's, showing the royal hatchment of 1700, and the Tudor font with late Jacobean cover and bracket.

London, and though fire is not mentioned, Samuel Pepys tells us that one of his contemporaries, Prince Rupert, saw the Great Fire of 1666 as a fulfilment of Mother Shipton's prophecies.

The first pamphlet to connect Mother Shipton with Knaresborough appeared in 1667, stating that she was born at 'Naseborough near the Dropping-Well in Yorkshire' in 1486 (though this was later changed to 1488). This pamphlet by Richard Head is clearly a piece of leg-pulling fantasy, describing Mother Shipton's devilish origin and supernaturally grotesque appearance, and contains many rhymed prophecies written in retrospect. For example:

Hell's Power by a fatal Blow
Shall seek the Land to overthrow

This purports to be Mother Shipton's prophecy of the Gunpowder Plot which, of course, had already taken place sixty-two years earlier.

Mother Shipton soon evolved from a harmless soothsayer, who may well have existed in the flesh,

25

Mother Shipton as portrayed in 1663, predicting the downfall of Wolsey. As this was in 1530, 'Old Mother Shipton' would have been forty-two at the time!

into a legendary witch. This is especially noticeable in the alleged portraits of her – a rather ordinary Tudor woman in 1641, but a hideous crone by 1663.

The printed prophecies also became more extravagant. For example:

Carriages without horses shall go
And accidents fill the world with woe.

True enough, and quite impressive as a prophecy if it had been written in Tudor times. But this was part of a Victorian forgery by a Brighton bookseller called Charles Hindley, who publicly acknowledged it in 1873. He also wrote the well-known lines:

The world then to an end shall come
In Eighteen-Hundred and Eighty-One.

The fact that it did not, made no difference to the credulous. The mythical witch-like profile was so well-known that 'Mother Shipton' seemed an obvious choice for the name of a moth with similar markings on its wings. By the beginning of the twentieth century the Mother Shipton industry was firmly established – though there is no hint in history that she was born in a cave. Curiously enough, in the early views of the Dropping Well there is no sign of a cave where one now exists, and until as recently as 1908 her birthplace was being shown as a house near Low Bridge.

One person we would have expected to refer to Mother Shipton was John Leland, the official antiquary appointed by Henry VIII. He came to Knaresborough in 1538, only a few years after the king had ordered Wolsey's arrest. But he made no mention of the prophetess, even though he paid particular attention to the Dropping Well, a unique cascade of petrifying water which coated porous objects with a calcareous deposit. It was already a tourist attraction, one of the oldest in the kingdom:

. . . a welle of a wonderful nature callid Droping welle. For out of the great rokkes by it distillith water continually into it. This water is so could and of such a nature that what thing so ever ys caste in, or growith about the rokke, and is touchid of this water, growith ynto stone.

Low Bridge, originally called March Bridge, and beyond it the
Mother Shipton Inn, also known as the Dropping Well.

Leland was equally impressed by the castle, which he described as standing 'magnificently and strongly on a rok'. He also commented that the rocky ground on which Knaresborough stands is the origin of its name.

Though Leland admitted that the market was 'quick' (lively), he thought the town itself 'meanely buildid'. This is borne out by the fact that Knaresborough has very few good buildings surviving from the Tudor period. We can, however, take pride in such gems as the thatched Manor Cottage at the foot of cobbled Water Bag Bank – so called because of the water carried up here in leather bags on the backs of donkeys and horses, and also by women doing horse-work, carrying buckets at a halfpenny a time. This water supply was supplemented by a number of wells in the town, the best surviving example of which is the Stock Well.

Below the cottage on the riverside is the Old Manor House, built round an ancient roof-tree, now concealed in a cupboard. Like the cottage this was for

The castle in Tudor times, from a sixteenth century drawing. We also see an impression of High Bridge, with the river flowing down to the weir and mill – the wrong direction!

Manor Cottage at the foot of Water Bag Bank. A drawing by Albert Walker.

St John's House at the end of Church Lane, one of the town's few Tudor buildings.

many years owned by the Roundell family, and is a house of great charm and character. The novelist Halliwell Sutcliffe said he had heard that Cromwell signed a treaty here with Charles I, but there seems to be no evidence to support this.

Another attractive Tudor building – both inside and out – is St John's House at the end of Church Lane, which has deeds going back to 1498. The Dower House across the road, though it has a Georgian exterior, has some Tudor work inside, as have several other buildings in High Street and in the market place. Two of the finest Tudor houses were both rebuilt in the eighteenth century. The first was Birnand Hall in York Place (now the Conservative Club), originally the home of the Birnand family. This family included John Birnand, in 1527 the King's Receiver for Knaresborough and Pontefract, and William Birnand, who served as Recorder for York from 1573 to 1582. Near here stood the Birnand Hall Cross, which seems to have been linked with the early administration of justice. The other important Tudor house was Coghill Hall, on the site of the present Conyngham Hall. This seat of the Coghill family, which included Sir John Coghill, Master of the High Court of Chancery in Ireland, was built by Marmaduke Coghill in 1555.

The market noted by Leland as a flourishing one must at first have been linked with the castle, whose garrison it would have supplied, but by this time it was the hub of a busy agricultural community surrounding the town. We know this from wills and inventories listing an abundance of cattle, sheep, pigs, poultry, wheat, oats, barley, rye and every kind of farming implement. The market was also noted for its locally-grown liquorice and, later, cherries – both probably having been introduced by medieval friars. Flax was also grown in the area, and in Tudor times we have the first indications of the cottage textile industry that was eventually to make Knaresborough linen famous. The names Tentergate and Tenter Lodge remind us of the

stretching of cloth on tenter hooks to dry, and the Old Dye House on Waterside goes back to the time of the successful dyer, John Warner, in the early seventeenth century.

Against the fairly stable background of the economy, there were all kinds of political and religious upheavals associated with the Reformation. In 1537, the year before the suppression of Knaresborough Priory, there was a recurrence of the protest movement of northern Catholics known as the Pilgrimage of Grace, as a result of which Henry VIII ordered the execution of about 200 people, including a number of local men, such as Lord Darcy, Steward of Knaresborough, and Sir Thomas Percy of Spofforth. By 1549 the parish church was Protestant, with services in Thomas Cranmer's clear and majestic English from the *Book of Common Prayer*, an emphasis on the Bible rather than liturgy, mass replaced by Holy Communion and the saints removed from their niches. The year 1553 was significant, not so much because it brought the reign of Mary Tudor and a temporary return to Catholicism, but because this was the year when Reginald Beisley and Ralph Scrope represented Knaresborough in Parliament, the first of the long line of MPs.

With the accession of Queen Elizabeth in 1558 the Protestant religion soon became firmly established, with the *Book of Common Prayer* and the Thirty-Nine Articles in use again by 1563. There was, however, a strong undercurrent of Catholic feeling in the district. In 1569, during the Rising of the North, rebels entered the parish church, destroyed the prayer books and briefly restored the Latin mass. Though Elizabeth now made it a crime to hear mass and treason to give shelter to a Catholic priest, both went on in secret, especially in the secluded village of Scotton just to the north-west of Knaresborough.

It was to Scotton that Guy Fawkes came to live when in his late teens. As far as is known, he was at that

Guido Fawkes

'Guye Fauxe of Scotton, gentilman', here seen in Spanish guise as a conspirator.

probably moved to nearby Percy House. This name reminds us of a powerful group of local families who remained staunchly Catholic, including the Percys of Spofforth, the Plumptons of Plumpton Hall, the Ingilbys of Ripley and the Trappes of Nidd. Through contact with recusants and through the influence of his stepfather, Guy Fawkes became a convert to the Catholic cause and – like many a convert – a zealot, with sufficient enthusiasm to go and enlist in the Spanish army, then fighting in the Netherlands. This explains why, though Guy once used to sign himself 'Guye Fauxe of Scotton, gentilman', he later called himself 'Guido' and had the Spanish appearance we see in his only known portrait.

He was, indeed, a gentleman rather than a mercenary villain, and was known for courageous service as a captain in the Spanish army, which is where he acquired an expertise in the use of gunpowder. We can imagine the sensation locally when news came of his attempt on the famous Fifth of November 1605 to blow up James I and his Parliament by means of the thirty-six barrels of gunpowder he had managed to smuggle into the vaults of the House of Lords.

Two Knaresborough men he might well have murdered if the Gunpowder Plot had succeeded were Sir Henry Slingsby and his brother Sir William, who were then serving as MPs. A visit to the remarkable Slingsby Chapel in the parish church immediately conveys an impression of loyal service to the Crown by this noble family connected with Scriven Hall. In the chapel we see the tomb bearing an effigy of the father of Henry and William, Francis Slingsby, reclining in full armour. He died in 1600 aged seventy-eight, after serving as a cavalry officer under Henry VIII and Queen Mary, and as Commissioner for Scotland under Queen Elizabeth. Lying on his right, because of her superior rank as a member of the Percy family, is his wife Mary, who died in 1598 aged sixty-six. Of their nine sons, the two who became MPs had

time a loyal Protestant. Born in York in 1570, he had been educated at St Peter's, a school closely associated with York Minster, where his father held an important legal post. When his father died, aged forty-six, Guy's mother remarried, this time to a Catholic, Dennis Bainbridge, a resident agent of Scotton, where she came to live with her family – Guy and his two sisters.

At first they lived in Scotton Old Hall – now said to be the oldest occupied house in England – and later

The Court of the Honour of Knaresborough in the Old Courthouse Museum. The scene shows a case in 1602 when Ann Lyster and Alice Prentice applied to exchange ownership of land.

distinguished careers, and are represented in the chapel by striking effigies.

Sir Henry Slingsby, knighted by King James in 1602, is shown in his burial shroud, rising from the dead on the Day of Judgement. (The men who broke down the wall to get his tomb into the chapel were treated to 'ayle and cakes' costing eighteen pence.) Though he was accused of mishandling the affairs of the Duchy of Lancaster and spent nearly two years in jail, he nevertheless did good work as Constable of the Castle and High Sheriff of Yorkshire. He died in 1634. His brother, Sir William Slingsby, who died in 1638, was a Commissary of the Fleet, who sailed with Drake against the Spanish Armada. His effigy depicts him as an officer in high-crowned hat, wearing boots and spurs, and resting on his sword.

Sir William Slingsby (died 1638), Commissary of the Fleet and MP for Knaresborough, as seen in the monument attributed to Epiphanius Evesham.

Recumbent effigies of Francis Slingsby (died 1600) and his wife Mary (died 1598). Behind is their son Sir Henry Slingsby (died 1634), depicted rising from the dead on the Day of Judgement.

King James's Grammar School (right) opened in 1616, rebuilt in 1741.

The establishment of a school in these unsettled times would have been seen as a stabilising and civilising influence, especially in an area associated with Guy Fawkes. This thought may well have occurred to King James when he was approached by the Rev Dr Robert Chaloner, Canon of Windsor, who had been born in Goldsborough, with a request for permission to found a school in Knaresborough. The letters patent were granted with unusual promptitude on the 26th October 1616 – only three weeks after Chaloner had applied for them. There still exists the original school charter bearing a portrait of King James, and a parchment scroll six feet long containing the original rules, or 'Ordinances and Lawes' for the 'Free Grammar School of King James'. Boys came from the parishes of Knaresborough and Goldsborough, and the schoolmaster was to 'take paines with all indifferently, as well poore as rich'. After a year, those pupils who were found to be 'unapt to learne' were to be taken from the school. Strict discipline was enforced, if necessary by means of 'a rod, moderately' or slaps across the hand with a ruler:

The Maister shall have diligent regard to the manners of his scholars, and see that they come not uncombed, unwashed, ragged or slovenly. But before all things he shall severely punish swearing, lying, picking, stealing, fighting and quarrelling, wanton speech and uncleane behaviour.

The 1616 charter of King James's Grammar School (right) with the
scroll of 'Ordinances and Lawes'.

Though schoolboy characteristics in 1616 have a familiar ring about them, the education system was very different. School started at six o'clock in summer, and seven in winter, with all the lads on their knees reciting Psalm 119 (the longest, with 176 verses!). As well as the fundamentals of the Christian faith, such as the Ten Commandments, the Apostles' Creed and the Catechism, the curriculum included a formidable amount of grammar, with the emphasis on correct spelling, punctuation and neat handwriting. For boys above the first form, all conversation was to be in Latin, even at playtime. Some relaxation was provided by the games period, consisting of instruction in archery.

Parents had to provide not only bows and arrows, but also paper, ink, pens, books and 'candles for winter'. They were solemnly ordered to see that their boys came to school on time, and were warned that they would be held responsible for any truancy:

If your childe shall use often to be absent from
the schoole, unlesse it be by reason of sickness,
he shall be utterly expelled from the schoole.

The school was closely connected with the parish church and occupied a house with a garden adjoining the churchyard, given by Peter Benson, a man of substance who owned sixteen burgage-houses, including one now named after the office he held – the Borough Bailiff Inn.

In addition to the founding of King James's Grammar School, the first half of the seventeenth century saw several instances of social improvement. They started in 1600 with the presentation of a robust new poor box (which can be seen in the church vestry, along with the parish register, with complete records of births, marriages and deaths from 1561 and boards recording several generous benefactions). Anthony Acham, for example, in 1638 left £6 to provide the poor with 'wheaten bread' six times a year 'so long as the world shall endure'. In 1647, Lord John Craven left £200 to benefit the poor of the town every Christmas. This money later helped to buy land at Scotton, producing the charity known as Scotton Rents, now part of Knaresborough Relief in Need. A more tangible benefaction, perhaps, was the building of almshouses for 'six poor folk' at the top of Kirkgate, mentioned in a survey of 1611, and still to be seen – unlike the almshouses that stood on the riverbank near High Bridge.

Rich and poor alike were soon to suffer under the turmoil brought by the reign of Charles I. When he finally allowed a Parliamentary election in 1640, Knaresborough became the scene of drunken rioting, and Henry Benson MP, son of the school's benefactor, was accused by his fellow MP, Sir Henry Slingsby (son of the first Sir Henry), of corruption, and was expelled from the Commons. The district was at this time being terrorised by wild and undisciplined Royalist soldiers based at the castle, restless because they had not been paid and living on credit or by plunder. This was a mere prelude to the Civil War, which was seen at its most ferocious at the Battle of Marston Moor, fought only ten miles from the town.

By the end of the 2nd July 1644, Oliver Cromwell and his Roundheads had won a decisive victory over the Royalist Cavaliers, at least 4,000 of whom were killed, including another tragic loss for the Plumpton family – John, son of Sir Edward. When the widow of one of the Royalist officers, Colonel Townley, rode from Knaresborough Castle to Marston Moor to search for her husband's body, she was courteously received by a Parliamentary officer who insisted on arranging an escort for her return. She was surprised to discover later that the officer was Cromwell himself. Yet the wrath of the Roundheads must have been dreaded in Knaresborough, the principal feature of which was its castle loyal to King Charles, from where

Prince Rupert had set out to confront Cromwell's army at Marston Moor.

They were kept in suspense until almost the end of the year. Then, on the 12th November, Cromwell's troops marched on Knaresborough, causing the Royalist soldiers to retreat into the castle with a loss of 20 killed, 48 wounded and 46 taken prisoner. The Parliamentarians are said to have kept their wounded in the parish church, where they also obliterated several pages of Royalist names in the parish register – though I know from forensic analysis that it was not done with blood, as tradition has maintained, and it is a pity to lose this macabre touch. They are also said to have stabled their horses in the church, and may well have vandalised it in other ways.

The besieging army of nearly 600 men was under the command of Colonel John Lilburne (by a rare coincidence the name of the rebel who had taken the castle in 1317), an officer who was to become well known as the leader of the Levellers. He made his first assault at the beginning of December, bombarding the walls from the top of Kirkgate with little effect. When he brought the artillery to the top of Briggate, the defenders sent out a raiding party through the southern sally-port (the one re-opened to the public in 1990), killing and wounding 42 of the Parliamentarians and taking 26 prisoners back into the castle. Two days later, cannonballs fired by the besiegers managed to breach the walls near the sally-port, and almost immediately the Royalists surrendered, even though they had 'a good store of arms, powder and ammunition . . . and almost £1,500 worth of plate, silver and gilt'.

Knaresborough Castle was taken on the 20th December 1644, officially surrendering to Lord Fairfax. Very little damage had been done to it, however, and – contrary to what modern visitors may imagine – its present ruined state is neither the result of the siege nor centuries of neglect. In fact it remained in all its glory for another four years – until 1648, when, as a result of an earlier Act of Parliament, it was one of the Royalist castles to be 'slighted' by systematic demolition.

Though Cromwell was not present during the siege, he certainly came to stay in Knaresborough, either shortly afterwards or in September 1648, when he may well have seen the destruction of the castle in progress. Many towns have a 'Cromwell slept here' claim, but Knaresborough has an eyewitness account of his stay in Cromwell House in High Street, preserved by Sir John Goodricke of Ribston Hall. He had heard it from an old lady who, as a young girl called Eleanor Ellis, had seen Cromwell when he stayed in her father's house. She had told him:

> Having heard much talk about the man I looked at him with wonder. Being ordered to take a pan of coals and air his bed, I could not forbear peeping over my shoulders several times to observe this extraordinary person, who was seated at the fireside, untying his garters. Having aired the bed I went out, and shutting the door after me, stopped and peeped through the keyhole, when I saw him rise from his feet, advance to the bed, and fall on his knees . . . When I returned again I found him still at prayer, and this was his custom every night so long as he stayed at our house.

This is interesting confirmation of Cromwell's piety, and also of the awe in which he was often held. Even when Cromwell House was rebuilt in 1764, the Protector was sufficiently venerated for the bedroom in which he had slept to be carefully preserved.

In spite of Knaresborough's Royalist associations, there must have been enthusiastic Parliamentarians in the town. In June 1645, for example, they managed to install their own vicar, Matthew Booth, stressing the democratic fairness of the procedure in a note in the

Pages from the parish register, showing vandalism by Cromwell's
soldiers – presumably the obliteration of Royalist names.

parish register. The following October, the town had a
new MP when a keen supporter of Cromwell, Thomas
Stockdale of Bilton Hall, replaced Sir Henry Slingsby,
who had been expelled from the House of Commons
in 1642 – only two years after he had achieved the
expulsion of Henry Benson.

Cromwell slept here – in the room above the archway – staying for
several days. A view from Whiteley's Yard, off High Street, by
Albert Walker.

Sir Henry ('Harry') Slingsby, a colonel in the Royalist army, beheaded on Tower Hill, the 8th June 1658, his headless body then being returned for burial in the parish church.

Sir Henry Slingsby – often called Sir 'Harry' to distinguish him from his father – was an ardent Royalist who detested Cromwell and all he stood for. He had taken steps to see that the castle was securely held for King Charles, and had fought on the losing side at Marston Moor, leaving an account of the battle in his diaries.

In 1654, on the tenth anniversary of the defeat, he joined hundreds of conspirators, including the Royalist secret society the Sealed Knot, on the battlefield. For his determination to restore Charles I he was arrested on a charge of high treason, imprisoned in Hull and later taken to be tried in London. There he was found guilty, and beheaded on Tower Hill on the 8th June 1658. Shortly before, he had written 'A Father's Legacy to his Sons', and also his own epitaph, which included the lines:

The Hatchet acted what the Court decreed,
Who would not for his HEAD lay down his Head?
Thus liv'd I, thus I dy'd; my Faith the wing
That mounts my Kingly zeal to th' Highest King.

Sir Henry Slingsby's headless body was brought back to Knaresborough, where it was placed in a tomb later covered by a simple slab of black marble, said to have come from St Robert's Priory. (The shirt in which he was executed can be seen in the Old Courthouse Museum). Part of the Latin inscription reads:

He suffered because of his faithfulness to his King and the law of the land. He has not perished, but has been translated to a better place, beheaded by the tyrant Cromwell.

With the dismantling of the castle in 1648, and now the ignominy of the execution of Sir Henry Slingsby as a traitor, this must have been a disquieting period for the people of Knaresborough. Yet they soon adapted to the changed circumstances. Stone from the castle was used to build many of the houses still seen today;

Scriven Hall, for centuries the home of the Slingsby family, drawn by Albert Walker before its demolition following the fire of 1952.

the Slingsby estates, including Scriven Hall and much of Knaresborough, which had been confiscated and sold by Cromwell, were recovered by his nephew Slingsby Bethel, who became MP for Knaresborough in 1658; and best of all, the economy of the town received a boost from an unexpected quarter.

This new source of income – later to change the face of the whole area – was inadvertently brought about by another member of the local Royalist family,

William Slingsby. Though he later moved to Bilton Hall, it was when he was living in a house near the Stray, in 1571, that he discovered a mineral spring of chalybeate water – soon to be widely known as the Tewit Well. Having travelled on the Continent, where he had tasted the water of such health resorts as Spa in the Ardennes, he realised the value of this spring, and was public-spirited enough to have the area paved and walled.

In about 1596 a physician called Timothy Bright was publicising this as 'the English Spa', and in 1626 a York physician, Edmund Deane, wrote a best-selling book *Spadacrene Anglica, or the English Spaw Fountaine*. This served as first-class publicity for Knaresborough, which Dr Deane commended with enthusiasm as the only place near the Tewit and other wells where suitable accommodation could be found. Writing while the castle was still in its prime, he had nothing but praise for this 'very ancient Market towne':

> Both the Castle and the Towne are fenced on the South and the West parts with the River Nid, which is beautiful here with two fair bridges of stone . . . About the towne are divers fruitful valleyes, well replenished with grasse, corne and wood. The waters there are wholesome and cleare, the ayre dry and pure. In brief, there is nothing wanting, that may fitly serve for a good and commodious habitation, and the content and entertainment of strangers.

Dr Deane recommended spa visitors to 'raise up their spirits for an hour or two' by walking round Knaresborough and to drink the petrifying water of the Dropping Well, which he claimed to be 'very effectual in staying any flux of the body'.(No doubt a useful antidote to the drastic laxative effect of the Harrogate sulphur water!)

Even before the Civil War there is clear evidence that Knaresborough had become a base for this new fashion of 'taking the waters', with visits from the gentry, military families and so many others, that in 1642 Sir Henry Slingsby had been advised to ensure that the town had a suitable vicar, in view of 'the great resort to it in summer-time by reason of the wells'. The reason health-seekers came here was that at this time Harrogate was no more than two separate hamlets, High Harrogate near the Tewit Well and St John's Well, and Low Harrogate, near the 'Stinking Spaw' or Old Sulphur Well.

Knaresborough's historic distinctions, incidentally, include one small item which tends to be overlooked. It was the first town in England to be associated with the name of Spa, in what is now Belgium. Even though Bath and Buxton are much older, and were known to the Romans, it was Knaresborough that first became linked with the newly-coined term 'spa'. This is shown first, by the title of a new edition of Deane's book published in 1649, *The English Spa, or the Glory of Knaresborough*; and, secondly, by the references which can be found to 'the Knaresborough Spaw' in the writings of diarists and travellers such as John Evelyn (1654), John Ray (1661), Oliver Heywood (1666), Ralph Thoresby (1692) and especially Celia Fiennes (1697). This famous side-saddle traveller relaxed in a Knaresborough garden amongst 'all manner of Curiosityes of Flowers and in a cherry garden with paths and viewpoints for visitors'. From here she went 'over to Haragate which is just by the Spaw, two miles further on a Common that belongs to Knaresborough, all marshy and wett'.

The spa was now being commended by various medical men, and though Dr Robert Wittie preferred Scarborough, it is interesting to note that, writing in 1669, he referred to Knaresborough and not to Harrogate in his top five spas:

> Let Epsom, Tunbridge, Barnet, Knaresborough be
> In what request they will, Scarborough for me.

Dr Wittie was rebuked the following year in a pamphlet by Dr George Tonstall, who declared that though he also had once preferred Scarborough he now found the Knaresborough spa much superior.

After the Restoration in 1660, a more relaxed atmosphere encouraged the development of all spas, the fashion being maintained by Charles II himself, who in 1684 spent a whole season at Epsom with his

A rare engraving of the Dropping Well in January 1739, when it
froze from top to bottom and visitors were able
to skate on the river.

court (and also Nell Gwynne). But though the closing years of the century continued to bring prosperity to Knaresborough's innkeepers and traders, there were signs that the spa trade would eventually become firmly established in the two Harrogate villages close to the wells. In 1687 the first inn was built in High Harrogate – the Queen's Head. This was followed by the opening of the Sinking Ship (later called the Royal Oak, then the Granby), and in Low Harrogate there appeared the Crown and the Old Swan, both dating from around 1700.

The Restoration also brought its problems, such as

the Act of Uniformity of 1662, when 2,000 Puritan ministers were ejected as Nonconformists. The Vicar of Knaresborough, Matthew Booth, conformed; but life cannot have been easy for Quakers, for example, three of whom had once noisily disrupted Booth's sermon in the parish church and had been imprisoned for eight weeks.

In 1666 the Quakers were greatly heartened by a visit from their leader, George Fox, who stayed at a house in Gracious Street. The Independents received their encouragement from Lady Hewley of Haya Park. They had not at first been able to worship

The Dropping Well in 1746. There is no sign of 'Mother Shipton's
Cave' in any of these early pictures.

regularly in Knaresborough, 'owing to the severe persecution of Nonconformists'. Then, in 1697, they converted a thatched barn on Windsor Lane into a chapel, apparently on land owned by Lady Sarah Hewley, who also provided a house there for the first minister, the Rev William Benson.

Knaresborough entered the eighteenth century having recovered from the loss of the castle. To some extent this had been compensated for by the town's role as a base for 'taking the cure'. In the early 1700s, visitors still tended to stay in Knaresborough and travel by carriage out to the Harrogate wells – a parallel found in Tunbridge and Tunbridge Wells. In 1717, for example, Daniel Defoe stayed in Knaresborough and, having visited the Dropping Well, went out to see the Harrogate wells. Defoe was surprised to find so many people drinking the waters in 'a most desolate out-of-the-world place'.

As the century progressed, however, accommodation and facilities near the wells developed to such an extent that visitors were staying in Harrogate and travelling in the reverse direction – out to Knaresborough, which was being recommended by spa physicians as the ideal place for exercise and relaxation amidst beautiful scenery. The market was also an attraction – by the end of the century the biggest corn market in Yorkshire, or so Hargrove claimed.

It was partly for the benefit of spa visitors that Sir Henry Slingsby (grandson of the Royalist) improved the walks and planted more trees in the Dropping Well Estate in about 1739. The very name 'Long Walk' is simply eighteenth century spa terminology. The distance between High Bridge and the Dropping Well is not particularly long, so this name must have been used to distinguish it from what they would surely have called the 'Short Walk' from Low Bridge, along which Slingsby planted a fine avenue of beech trees, still to be seen. Sir Henry, who was MP for Knaresborough during four successive Parliaments, was married to the daughter of John Aislabie of Studley, Chancellor of the Exchequer. He seems to have allowed access to the Dropping Well, not only to his aristocratic friends but also to the general public, all the year round, as various contemporary engravings show. An anonymous writer from this period describes how he and his friends had to:

> . . . leave with Reluctance a Place where Nature has elegantly disposed every Ingredient she could bestow to form a chearful and pleasing Scene . . . the venerable Ruins of a large Castle, and a charming Intermixture of Rocks and Trees on the opposite Hill.

In addition to the landscaping of the Long Walk, other improvements to the town mark the increasing prosperity during the eighteenth century. From 1720 we can imagine health-seekers and hypochondriacs making use of the apothecary's in the market place, where John Beckwith dispensed remedies ranging from herbal potions to quills filled with quicksilver, the latter reputed to keep both disease and witches at bay. Bearing the undisputed title of the Oldest Chemist's Shop in England, this has been in continuous use as a pharmacy ever since, run by the Lawrences, father and son, for more than a hundred years, until Mr W P Lawrence retired in 1965. It still retains an eighteenth century atmosphere, with its oak beams, bleeding-couch, leech jar, mortar and pestle (once turned by a dog), antique drawers and bottles, and Old English Lavender Water, still made on the premises to the traditional secret recipe.

To meet the spiritual needs of inhabitants and visitors alike, various improvements were made in the parish church. In 1730 box pews replaced the earlier rough benches, and a massive three-decker pulpit was installed. From this a record number of sermons must have been preached by the Rev Thomas Collins MA, the town's longest-serving vicar, who was incumbent here from 1735 until his death in 1788 at the age of eighty-four. His contribution to the welfare of the district is incalculable, but tangible evidence of it includes a chapel-of-ease built in High Harrogate in

Knaresborough House (1768) in its delightful grounds, as seen from Collins Court.

The eight bells of the parish church with the original inscriptions. This view, taken after they had been recast in 1925, shows on the left the vicar, Canon H L Ogle, with the parish clerk, Charles Inman.

1749, later to be rebuilt as Christ Church, the building of Knaresborough House as his home, probably by John Carr of York (1768), the installation of eight bells (1774) in the parish church, made by Peake and Chapman of London, the total cost of more than £500 being reduced by the melting down of four existing bells, said to have come from the priory, and the installation of the first known organ of St John's, costing £276, and raised by public subscription (1788). The bells, though recast in 1925, still have the original inscriptions, and bell-ringing practice every Tuesday night happily maintains the tradition of guiding drovers and traders to the town on the eve of market day by the sound of the bells.

John Wesley, who visited the town six times.

The Rev Thomas Collins also had a responsibility for King James's Grammar School – which was rebuilt on the same site in 1741 – as well as helping to administer various charities, such as those of Andrew Holden (1707) and William Roundell (1729). Knaresborough also had one of the earliest of the Friendly Societies, meeting in 1745 as the Royal Foresters, though not officially established here until 1813 by John Smithson, a Quaker flax-dresser.

In 1765 the Charity School was established by Thomas Richardson for 'thirty boys and girls of the township of Knaresborough, and for putting them out to apprentice'. It can still be seen towards the bottom of High Street, with the names of the first benefactors plainly displayed.

Spiritual and educational work was also being done by the Methodists, who can trace their origins to the first two visits of the famous horseback evangelist, John Wesley, in 1742. He came again on four other occasions, always finding a warm reception for his preaching of the Gospel, so much so that in 1744 his sermon was once interrupted by a rowdy drunk, and on his last visit in 1761 he recorded of the mob that crowded into the Assembly Room in Savage Yard: 'Most of the people looked wild enough when they came in, but they were tame before they went out'. The Methodists built a bigger meeting house at Bond End in 1794, organised preaching throughout the Knaresborough Circuit of village chapels and, along with other denominations, helped to give the elementary education provided by the Sunday schools, started in Knaresborough on the 30th January 1785 with 473 children, all supported by generous public subscription.

In contrast to these benevolent educators, mention must be made of the schoolmaster hanged and gibbeted for murder, Eugene Aram. Born at Ramsgill in Upper Nidderdale in 1704, he settled in Knaresborough in 1734, opening a school in White Horse Yard – now Park Square, where only the cobbles survive. Though remarkably studious and erudite, he became closely acquainted with a rough flax-dresser, Richard Houseman, whose heckling shop was adjacent to the school. In February 1745 a young shoemaker called Daniel Clark, who had recently amassed a quantity of valuable goods on credit, disappeared and was assumed to have absconded. He was last seen alive in the company of Aram and Houseman. Soon afterwards the schoolmaster paid off his debts and left the town.

More than thirteen years later – in August 1758 – as a result of the chance discovery of a skeleton on Thistle Hill, Houseman confessed that the remains of Daniel Clark were not these bones, but would be found in St Robert's Cave, where he had seen Eugene Aram strike him down. When a second skeleton was found in the cave, the two Knaresborough constables were immediately sent to King's Lynn, where Aram was

Frontage of the Oldest Chemist's Shop, showing the box windows
on legs of the 'Chinese Chippendale', added around 1760.

Inside the Oldest Chemist's Shop, showing formularies, leech-jar, pill-making machine, medicine bag, bottle-tree and apothecary's drawers.

Richardson's Charity School in High Street, founded in 1765.

Eugene Aram's school in White Horse Yard with Richard Houseman's heckling shop on the right (1745).

teaching in the grammar school. He was arrested, brought back to Knaresborough and then transferred to York Castle, where he was imprisoned for a year. At his trial at the York Assizes on the 3rd August 1759, in spite of his impressive, scholarly defence he was found guilty and condemned to be hanged in York, his body then to be displayed on the Knaresborough gibbet, which stood a little above the Mother Shipton Inn. Though Houseman, who had turned king's evidence, was clearly an accomplice, and though there was a certain amount of sympathy for the schoolmaster (the Rev Thomas Collins collected £5 for him when he was in prison), I can only say that my own research of this complex case led me to the conclusion that Eugene Aram was deeply involved in Clark's murder.

Eugene Aram, hanged for murder on the 6th August 1759.

John Metcalf, better known as 'Blind Jack', as he looked in 1795.

school, John Metcalf lost the sight of both eyes through an attack of smallpox, a disease which various sources show to have been common in Knaresborough at this time. Undaunted by this affliction, he seemed all the more determined to lead the life of a normal, lively lad, climbing trees, swimming in the Nidd, becoming an expert horseman and even a huntsman. Blind though he was, young Metcalf could always find his way around, and soon he was being employed as a guide – especially useful at night and in fog, when a sighted person would inevitably be handicapped.

He also proved to be a good musician, and from the age of fifteen was playing his fiddle for spa visitors, especially in the Royal Oak at Harrogate, where he fell in love with the landlord's daughter and eventually eloped with her, remaining happily married for forty years. He also played the oboe, which was no doubt the instrument he mostly used when he became musician to the Knaresborough Volunteers, the seventy men led by Captain William Thornton, when they marched north to fight Bonnie Prince Charlie's rebels in July 1745, and for whom the parish church bells were rung to celebrate the victory of Culloden.

Blind Jack was as versatile as he was energetic and enterprising. He tried his hand at horse-dealing, worked as a carrier and fishmonger, ran a stagecoach between Knaresborough and Harrogate, and also engaged in a great deal of gambling and a certain amount of smuggling. His fame, of course, rests on road-building, which has earned him a place in many a history book alongside such pioneers as Macadam and Telford. This was one of his later ventures, started in 1765 when he was forty-eight, but he went on from his first three mile stretch between the villages of Minskip and Ferrensby to build hundreds of miles of road throughout the North of England, as well as bridges. The viameter he used to measure distances can be seen in the museum, and we can imagine him trundling this along his newly-completed turnpike roads, checking

More wholesome and more inspiring is John Metcalf, better known as 'Blind Jack' – in my view the greatest of Knaresborough's characters. Born in 1717, he was contemporary with Eugene Aram – though he can hardly have been telling visitors the story of the crime when still a boy (as one writer has assumed) some thirty years before it came to light! At the age of six, when he had fortunately already had two years at

Blind Jack's mug and one of his sticks, held by the author near the site of the Metcalf home.

The viameter owned by 'Blind Jack'. Trundled over hundreds of miles of new roads, its special dial enabled him to measure distances by touch.

the surface with his stick, his lively personality and formidable appearance – six feet two inches and seventeen stone – a constant inspiration to his gangs of workmen. He died in his ninety-third year in 1810 at the home of one of his daughters in Spofforth, where we can read on his gravestone:

Here lies John Metcalf, one whose infant sight
Felt the dark pressure of an endless night . . .
'Twas his a guide's unerring aid to lend;
O'er trackless wastes to bid new roads extend . . .

The second half of the eighteenth century saw not only the provision of badly-needed roads but many structural improvements in Knaresborough itself. We can note, for example: the enlargement of High Bridge, then known as Danyell Bridge (1773), and Low Bridge (1779); and the rebuilding of the Borough courthouse, the Sessions House or tollbooth, with two prison cells beneath (1768), which the prison reformer John Howard later found to be infested with rats from the open sewers. There was a new chapel on Windsor Lane 'for Protestant Dissenters, commonly called Presbyterians', later Congregationalists (1779); and a number of fine Georgian houses, especially those in

York Place, where William Manby rebuilt Birnand Hall (1780). In its favoured position down by the river, Coghill House, already rebuilt – probably by John Carr – was restored and extended by Ellen, Dowager Countess of Conyngham, henceforth to be known as Conyngham Hall (1796).

Further down the river, a more humble dwelling was taking shape: the House in the Rock, made between 1770 and 1791 by a weaver and his son. In a superb position near the Crag Chapel, it soon became a tourist attraction, where spa visitors came to take tea and see the eccentric owner, styled by his admirers 'Sir' Thomas Hill, flying a Union Jack from the battlements

The 'Woolley Headed Boy', a young guide with hair like a fleece, who could be found at the House in the Rock around 1795.

The Birnand Hall Cross as it appeared in the eighteenth century. The site is marked by a brass cross near the rebuilt hall in York Place.

of his 'Fort Montague' (named in honour of his benefactress, the Duchess of Buccleugh, a friend of the Slingsbys), and occasionally firing a salute from his two pounder cannon. Here they also had the services of an unusual guide, another of Knaresborough's forgotten characters. When the artist Joseph Farington went to see St Robert's Cave he noted: 'We were attended to this spot by a Boy, called the Woolley Headed Boy, his Hair having that appearance and texture.'

Coghill Hall in 1788, the seat of Sir John Coghill, restored and
enlarged as Conyngham Hall in 1796.

An 1830 view of the House in the Rock, or 'Fort Montague', from
Spitalcroft.

'Sir' Thomas Hill, 'Governor of Fort Montague' – or the House in the Rock, completed on the 10th January 1791.

A special Act of Parliament in 1764 brought great benefit: the pumping of water from the Nidd, conveyed up into the town by means of wooden pipes until about 1785, when they were replaced by leaden ones. This must have been welcomed by the early fire brigade, vital in those days when so many of the town's houses were thatched. The brigade certainly existed in 1774, the date of the fire engine in the museum. This used to be kept behind the inn now called the Borough Bailiff, where the fire bell can still be seen. The firemen were unpaid volunteers, usually from appropriate trades such as plumbers, blacksmiths and joiners.

In 1770 a small paper mill was built next to the pumping station, with which it shared the weir. In 1790 a new and bigger waterwheel was constructed, and the following year a large cotton mill was built on the same site, soon to be known as Castle Mill. The staple industry, however, was the manufacture of linen, at this time still being carried on in cottages and small workshops scattered throughout the town, and it was only a matter of time before the new mill was converted to the spinning of flax and the weaving of some of the best-quality linen in the country.

At one time the fields around Knaresborough would have been blue with the delicate flowers of flax, but this was gradually replaced by imports from the Baltic, 2,300 tons coming through Hull in 1783, much of it destined for Lower Nidderdale. Writing in 1787, Hargrove observed that the linen trade was 'in a flourishing condition', with more than 1,000 pieces of linen (20 yards by 35 inches) manufactured in the town and neighbourhood every week. In 1811 the mill changed from cotton to flax, and by 1830 had 120 workers, includind 47 children aged from 10 to 16.

In 1847, Castle Mill was taken over by Walton and Company, who had been established since 1785. Their linen was of such fine quality that in 1838, the second year of Queen Victoria's reign, Waltons was appointed linen manufacturers to the royal household, and was later able to advertise 'Knaresborough Linens, now used in all the royal palaces', weaving into their exclusive tea-towels, names such as Sandringham, Balmoral and Buckingham Palace. By 1851 they had increased their workforce to 423, and it was in this year at the Great Exhibition in London that the firm

An early nineteenth century view of the Dropping Well, with Low
Bridge and Fort Montague in the distance.

received the Prince Albert Medal for the seamless linen shirt woven by George Hemshall.

The success of Waltons might give a mistaken impression of Victorian prosperity. But beneath Knaresborough's picturesque and romantic exterior, widely publicised through such influential books as John Bigland's *The Beauties of England and Wales* (1812), and still attracting crowds of visitors from the rapidly developing spa of Harrogate, there lay dire poverty and insanitary squalor, in urgent need of attention. A start had been made in 1823, when an Act of Parliament authorised a body of improvement commissioners who, by levying an 'improvement rate' of one shilling and sixpence, undertook to set about the 'paving, lighting, watching, cleansing and improving of Knaresborough'.

A tranquil view, drawn in about 1783. Notice the thatched
parsonage in front of the church, demolished in 1870.

An engraving of Turner's watercolour of Knaresborough (1826)
showing Castle Mill (left) and (centre) a man laying out linen to
bleach.

Plate opposite
Labels used by Waltons showing the royal arms,
the Prince Albert Medal and 'Knaresborough linens
now used in all the royal palaces'.

The seamless linen shirt woven by George Hemshall on a
handloom at Castle Mill, which won the Prince Albert Medal at the
Great Exhibition of 1851.

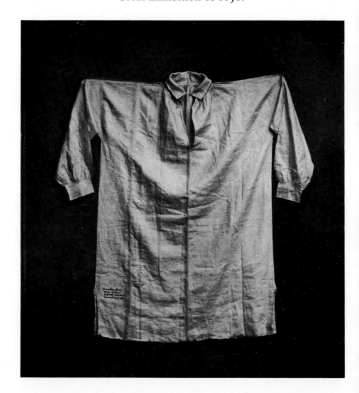

The Rev William Howell, Congregationalist minister from 1782
until 1835, apart from a year's absence as a missionary, when he
was twice captured at sea.

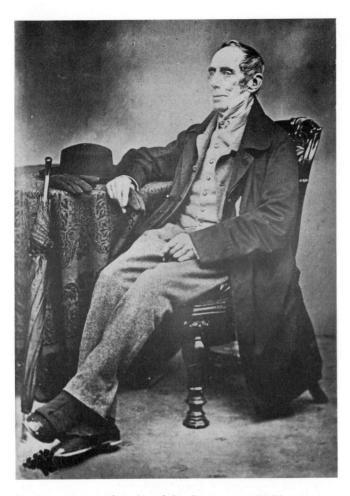

Dr Peter Murray, founder of the dispensary, a highly-respected physician in the town from 1803 to 1826.

The most successful aspect of their work was the provision of street lighting. John Malam was appointed as engineer, and by the 13th September 1824 he had the first gas-lamps lit – only a year after the establishment of the improvement commissioners. With one of the earliest provincial gasworks in the country, Knaresborough had a total of 129 public gas-lamps by 1864. As a kind of symbol of its success, the market cross, badly eroded since its renewal in 1708, was replaced by a gas-lamp, seen in all the early photographs.

Less successful was the attempt of the commissioners to improve cleanliness and hygiene. With sewage still being dumped into the Nidd, it is not surprising that the water-borne disease of cholera appeared in the town in 1832, killing thirty-two people. It struck again the day before Christmas Eve 1848, and within a few weeks there were thirty-eight deaths. Even when the commissioners installed the town's first real sewers in 1850 – as distinct from open drains and ditches – the effluent still went into the river. Dunghills abounded, and High Street was fouled every week by the cattle market held there (and was not moved to a permanent site until 1907).

Long before the commissioners appointed their first medical officer in 1873, doctors had been toiling away in the public interest, notably Peter Murray, who had qualified as an MD at Edinburgh when only nineteen. He took up his work in Knaresborough in 1803, where he became 'the constant friend of the poor, and the active supporter of every good work', staying here for twenty-three years, after which he retired to Scarborough because of his own ill-health. Dr Murray founded the Dispensary for Free Medicine at the top of Castle Ings. In 1853 a new dispensary was built in Castle Yard as a memorial to another of the town's invaluable vicars, the Rev Andrew Cheap, incumbent from 1804 to 1851.

The Dispensary for Free Medicine, built in 1853 as a memorial to
the Rev Andrew Cheap.

The Rev Andrew Cheap was not only a trustee of the dispensary, but also the champion of the poor in many other ways, administering various charities, such as those created by Mrs Alice Shepherd (1806), William Yates (1807), Dr William Craven (1812) and Henry Hopps (1832), the latter providing seventy-eight twopenny loaves to be distributed 'amongst the poor of Knaresborough on January 1st for ever'. The vicar had oversight of the workhouse (originally near the church and rebuilt in 1858 in Stockwell Road, later to become the hospital) which in 1832 had fifty-one inmates. The poor were also helped through the Female Society (for pregnant women) and the Penny Club, mainly providing blankets. It was through the influence of the Rev Andrew Cheap that the two National Schools were built – first Castle Boys' School in 1814, then Castle Girls' School in 1837. In 1823 Charles Marshall left £500 to provide 'complete suits of clothing, at Easter, for two boys and two girls, being the best scholars' – the tradition of awarding 'Marshall suits' still being maintained at Castle Junior School, though now as the equivalent in money.

The Church of England was not the only denomination to contribute to the educational needs of the town. The Methodists, who had built their first real chapel in 1815 (the year of Waterloo) on the site of a cherry orchard in Gracious Street, ran a successful 'Sabbath and Day School' there, with its own library. Records show that in 1842, for example, the Methodists were giving elementary education to 170 pupils, 'mostly children who had no other means of receiving instruction'. Children were also being taught by the Catholics at St Mary's School in Bond End, which in 1851 had 102 boys and 95 girls, the latter praised by an inspector for their proficiency in reading and writing, and the fact that their 'peculiarity of tone or accent had been almost entirely removed'. This attempt to suppress local speech would presumably not have pleased the schoolmaster David Lewis,

originally of Belmont Farm, who in 1815 had been one of the earliest to publish poems – which he had written – in local Yorkshire dialect.

In addition to the denominational schools and King James's, there were several private schools in the town, including one in Gracious Street run by Thomas Cartwright. It was here that William Stubbs, born in 1825 above the entrance to Berry's Passage, received his early education before moving to Ripon Grammar School. Proud of his birth in a historic town and of a long line of ancestors there, William Stubbs became famous as a professor of medieval history at Oxford, as well as Canon of St Paul's, then Bishop of Chester and, in 1889, Bishop of Oxford. The Victorian painter W P Frith, born at Studley in 1819, also received his early education in Knaresborough, though it has not been possible to identify the school, which he described as 'of the Dotheboys Hall pattern'.

William Stubbs (1825–1901), the Knaresborough-born medieval historian who became a Canon of St Paul's, Bishop of Chester and Bishop of Oxford.

Victorian Knaresborough was a community of Christians, with most of the population at worship on Sundays. Evidence of this comes, first, from a census of 1851 which recorded 2,047 Anglicans, 843 Methodists, 227 Congregationalists, 105 Baptists and 250 Roman Catholics. Secondly, there were new church buildings appearing all over the town: St Mary's Catholic Church (1831), the Primitive Methodist chapel and town mission in Briggate (1854), a new Wesleyan Methodist chapel adjacent to the 1815 building, partly through a donation from Isaac Holden, the Liberal MP (1868), and a new Congregational church in Windsor Lane (1864). The parish church underwent a radical restoration, completed in 1872, by which time the chancel roof had been raised to its original height, windows – called the clerestory – added to the nave, and several stained-glass windows installed, including two by Morris & Co. The clock in the tower was not renewed until 1884, when an existing wooden face was kept (replaced by a fibreglass replica in 1975), bearing St Paul's exhortation to use the present opportunity to the full:

Redeeming the Time

By 1872, new oak pews had replaced the old box pews and galleries, no longer needed since the creation in 1856 of a new parish with its own church.

This was Holy Trinity Church, built at a cost of £3,800 to the design of John Fawcett in a modern Early Decorated style. It contains a font of Caen stone – donated by the Knaresborough-born Rev Dr William Kay, one of the revisers of the Old Testament – and an east window depicting scenes from the life of Jesus, which was unveiled at a memorial to Prince Albert on the 14th December 1862. The most impressive feature of Holy Trinity is the spire, which contains a single bell donated by the MP, Basil T Woodd. The spire is 166 feet tall, and as the church is built at the highest

St Mary's Roman Catholic Church, Bond End, built in 1831 – nicknamed 'the Gate of Heaven' from words once inscribed on the gable. The roadside Calvary is a war memorial.

Holy Trinity Church as it appeared soon after its consecration in 1856. Designed by Joseph Fawcett, its best-known feature is the spire, 166 feet tall.

point of the town it can be seen for miles around, a familiar landmark to guide Knaresborians home.

For visitors as well as residents, however, the best-known landmark is the railway viaduct, built in 1851. It is now so much an essential part of the scene that we forget that Knaresborough was even more picturesque without it – as can be seen, for example, in the lithographs of Samuel Howell, son of the Congregationalist minister, the Rev William Howell. This was what the architectural authority Niklaus Pevsner had in mind when he described the way the Victorians allowed the railway to cut through the heart of the town as 'one of the most notable railway crimes of England'. On the other hand, J B Priestley greatly admired the way the viaduct harmonised with the landscape. It gave, he said, 'a double beauty to the scene ... the graceful, ornamented arches were clearly reflected in the water'. Most would agree with him, though on the rare occasions when a steam train passes over it, we are reminded that the purpose of the viaduct was not to improve the scenery, but to link Knaresborough with the railway network so it would have better commercial prospects, as well as a cheaper supply of coal.

The first attempt had been a resounding disaster. Designed by Thomas Grainger for the East and West Yorkshire Junction Railway, the viaduct had been started in 1847, the foundation stone having been laid amidst great celebration and witnessed by all the schoolchildren on the 5th April by Joseph Dent of Ribston Hall, High Sheriff of Yorkshire. This gigantic structure, 338 feet long, 90 feet high with 4 arches of 56 foot spans, was almost completed when, shortly after noon on Saturday the 11th March 1848, it collapsed into the river, the arches on the Long Walk side falling down five minutes after the others. Tom Collins, who became MP for Knaresborough in 1851, and was later Deputy Lieutenant of the West Riding, narrowly escaped being crushed to death; but there was no loss

Knaresborough before the viaduct. Samuel Howell's view from
'the castle rock' in 1836.

Steam trains still use the 1851 railway viaduct. A class 5 locomotive
on its way to York.

The railway viaduct, completed in 1851 following its collapse in 1848. It is 90 feet high, 338 feet long, with four arches of 56 foot spans.

'Noisy Tom', the Knaresborough MP once described as the 'arch-interrupter of the House of Commons'. Thomas Collins, a barrister, was elected Conservative MP for the town in 1851, 1857, 1859 and 1881.

of life except to fish killed by the lime in the mortar. Apparently the structure had been weakened by heavy rain, and there were the contributory factors of poor workmanship and shoddy materials, as well as too hasty a removal of the scaffolding. A contemporary account says of the collapse:

> The sight was one of awful grandeur, the timber staging and an immense quantity of timber in the centreings, were literally smashed to atoms, and nearly all the stones are broken into slivers.
> The debris caused the water to back a considerable way up the river.

The damming of the Nidd, in fact, caused the water to rise twelve feet, flooding homes and covering Waterside with mud. But eventually, after many disputes, the mess was cleared and the viaduct carefully rebuilt by the contractor George Wilson and his 270 workmen at a cost of £9,803. The station was also completed, and the line to York opened on the 1st October 1851.

Amongst other sensations which shook the town in the nineteenth century, two have lasting memorials. First, there were the Castle Yard Riots of 1865, a public protest against Dr John Simpson, who lived next to Castle Girls' School and who had fenced off the right of way down past the castle to the river. Led by a tailor called William Johnson, attempts had been made over several years to break open the locked gates, and Simpson, who was a JP, had once struck Johnson with a stick before being restrained by Sergeant Archy of the police. Eleven men, including Johnson, were arrested and imprisoned for three months. So strong was the feeling that they had been made martyrs for acting in the public interest, that on their release each of them was presented with a silver tankard, some still treasured in the town. The tankards carry an inscription praising the men for 'asserting the rights of the public against the agression of Dr John Simpson'.

The silver tankard presented to Joseph Kearton on the 26th June 1866, one of eleven given to each of the men imprisoned after the Castle Yard Riots.

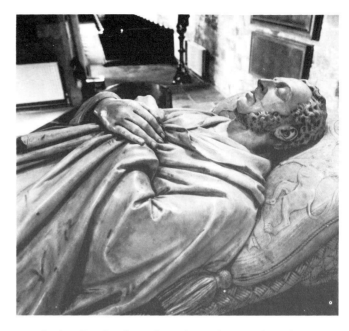

Sir Charles Slingsby, from the sculpture by Joseph Boehm on his tomb in the Slingsby Chapel.

The other sensation occurred four years later. This was the tragic death by drowning of Sir Charles Slingsby, last of the male line. During a foxhunt on the 4th February 1869, he was crossing the River Ure near Newby Hall when the ferryboat capsized, resulting in the death of six men and eight horses. The memorials to Sir Charles, in addition to the evergreen oak he planted at Scriven when he came of age, are the recumbent effigy on his tomb in the parish church, and the west window, both given by his sister Emma Louisa Catherine.

Victorian Knaresborough must have been dominated by the constant awareness of the way its once insignificant neighbour was rapidly outgrowing it. In 1821, High Harrogate had a population of 1,583 and Low Harrogate 1,010 – a total only half

The funeral cortege of Sir Charles Slingsby arriving at the west
door of the parish church on Thursday the 11th February 1869.
There were at least 1,150 mourners on foot, as well as 10 coaches
carrying dignitaries, and 53 private carriages.

Sir Charles Slingsby with the York and Ainsty Hounds in the sport
that was to lead to his tragic death in 1869. This painting now hangs
in Knaresborough House.

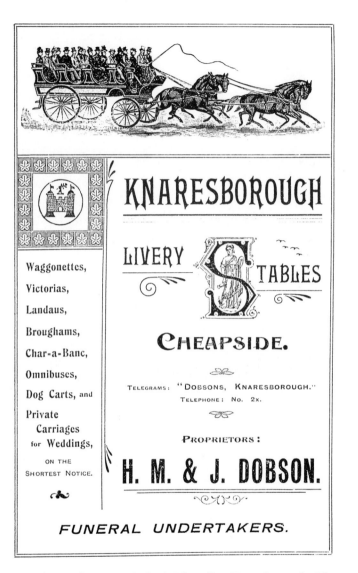

An advert of 1906 typical of Edwardian Knaresborough. The symbol based on a seventeenth century seal of the Honour of Knaresborough was now in common use.

Knaresborough's population of 5,283. By 1891, whereas Knaresborough remained about the same with 6,742 inhabitants (including Scriven), Harrogate had mushroomed to a population of 17,835 and reached nearly 30,000 by the end of the century. Added to this was a steady increase in visitors to the spa – rising from 20,586 in 1839 to 26,700 in 1848. Many of these came to Knaresborough as part of their therapy, but nothing could alter the fact that Harrogate, whose two villages had now merged to form a prosperous town, had an economy soundly based on the wells in its midst, and was becoming the major employer of the area. In Knaresborough, with the exception of Walton's Castle Mill, employment was typically in small concerns, such as the Rope Walk on Crag Top, owned by the Johnson family at the end of the century.

Apart from the Dropping Well, whose suspended petrifactions naturally discouraged medicinal use of the water, the nearest mineral springs to Knaresborough were at Starbeck. However, an Enclosure Act of 1778 had included these within the Knaresborough boundary, and in 1822 a committee was formed to revive the Old Spa. New buildings (some still to be seen) were started the following year, and it was renamed the Knaresborough Spa. The water was used for both drinking and bathing, and there were ten bathrooms 'neatly fitted up with every requisite convenience for Warm, Shower, and Cold Bathing'. The Knaresborough Spa was supported by Dr Murray and enthusiastically promoted by a Knaresborough chemist and local historian, Michael Calvert, who remained secretary and treasurer to the spa trust from 1822 until 1849.

The imaginative venture of conveying sulphur water into Knaresborough itself was made in 1887 to mark the golden jubilee of Queen Victoria. The improvement commissioners set up a special jubilee committee, which arranged for the water to be piped

Knaresborough Spa, advertised as 'midway between Harrogate and Knaresborough'. Dating from 1828, it was extended in the 1830s and 1840s, offering mild sulphur water and chalybeate water for both drinking and bathing.

from a sulphur well near Bilton Hall down to a stone fountain set up opposite the George Hotel (now the Yorkshire Lass). The sulphur water was highly commended by doctors and the chemists commissioned to analyse it, and promoted as 'an important addition to the attractions of Knaresborough as a health resort', being available there until about 1947. The Dropping Well Estate maintained the fountain as a flower container for some years, but in 1984 removed this interesting item of Knaresborough's heritage to private land.

Accounts of the jubilee celebrations show that the townspeople, whatever their economic difficulties, certainly knew how to enjoy themselves. For example, the jubilee committee decreed that 'all poor people above the age of 68 (that being the age of her Most Gracious Majesty) be entertained to a meat tea'. Later the age limit was reduced to sixty-five, and there were 290 applications for tickets. On Tuesday the 20th June 1887, all Knaresborough was astir with what were known as 'The Rejoicings'. The proceedings opened with 'the firing of a Royal Salute from the Russian Gun'. This once-famous novelty was a twenty-four pounder cannon captured at Sebastopol in the Crimean War, presented to the town in 1857. It was eventually situated near where the war memorial now stands – an ideal position for firing harmless blanks of turf and booming out over the Nidd gorge. Then, to the ringing of church bells, there were processions through streets festooned with flags to the crowded market place, where there were speeches, the National Anthem and *Rule Britannia*, followed by a free tea for the children, a cricket match and a firework display in the castle grounds.

Festivities of this kind were not confined to royal occasions. Victorian and Edwardian Knaresborough not only had popular 'Traders' Processions', but also became famous for what was styled 'England's Unique Water Pageant'. This annual Water Carnival was based on the popular industry of boating on the Nidd, where two excellent firms – Sturdys and Blenkhorns – exploited unrivalled facilities for rowing, punting and canoeing, all amidst glorious scenery. The first known person to provide boats for hire was William Bluett, a custodian of the castle, who died in 1850. He was followed by Richard Sturdy of Richmond House, whose landing stages and boat-building workshop were just below the castle; and Charles Blenkhorn near High Bridge, where he was publican of the World's End and who in 1900 opened the New Century Dining Rooms. (Charles Blenkhorn was also the postmaster, following in the footsteps of Mrs Henrietta Parr, said to have been England's very first postmistress.) Whereas Blenkhorns was licensed for 90 pleasure boats, Sturdys was a larger concern with 140 boats, and his territory formed the auditorium for the Water Carnival, with rows of seats (built by Kitchings) along Waterside and spectators crowding Castle Bank above.

The stage was the river itself, from the viaduct to Castle Mill, the opposite bank in the Dropping Well Estate being used for a special set piece, such as an illuminated fairy castle, for the main part of the Water Carnival was at night, and its climax was a spectacular fireworks display by Brocks, with fire raining down from the viaduct to imitate Niagara Falls. (In 1903, for example, this cost £58.) An essential component was the houseboat, the *Marigold*, owned by the O'Reilly sisters, with a band playing on its upper deck. There was a procession of illuminated and decorated boats led by the 'Fairy Queen of the Carnival' (the ancestor of the queen still crowned on Children's Day), with more music, including mandolin bands, pierrots and glee choirs on floating platforms of punts or boats tied together, and dancing, especially by the children. The carnival was perhaps at its best in the years before the First World War, when George Smith of Sturdys, who normally operated the 'penny ferry', had the job of setting up thousands of fairy lights in the riverside

The Water Carnival in 1903 – a rare postcard showing the Fairy Palace, the Eiffel Tower, the houseboat *Marigold* and the fireworks display by Brocks, including 'Niagara Falls' from the viaduct.

trees, when Jim Kell designed the flower-bedecked floats and boats, and when Don Pedro did his hair-raising tightrope walk across the gorge, pushing a man across in a wheelbarrow.

The houseboat *Marigold*, a popular cafe in the early 1900s. Note the typical canoes and Waltons linen mill.

Though it could muster a carnival atmosphere and had a strong sense of community, Knaresborough no longer held its former status. As a result of an Act of Parliament disfranchising small boroughs, it had lost the right to elect even the single MP to which it had already been reduced, a historic decision announced in this mock obituary notice:

In Affectionate Remembrance of
The Electoral Borough of
KNARESBOROUGH
who after an Existence of 332 Years, 1 Month
and 9 Days, during which time this Borough
Returned 187 Members to the House of Commons
Departed this Life
on Wednesday, November 18th, 1885.

In 1894 the improvement commissioners were replaced by the Knaresborough Urban District Council, which had fifteen elected members who appointed a town clerk, treasurer, surveyor and inspector of nuisances, market toll collector, gas foreman, sewage farm manager and medical officer. The first chairman of the KUDC was Basil T Woodd JP, of Conyngham Hall. A barrister, he had first been elected Conservative MP for Knaresborough in 1852, and was easily re-elected on five subsequent occasions. There can be no doubt that he made an outstanding contribution to the welfare of the town, and that in the words inscribed on the memorial organ-case in the parish church (1897), he was 'a bright example of life well spent in the service of Church and State'. Other chairmen of the council worthy of special mention are Thomas Stead JP, who held the office for thirteen years in succession (1904–16); Henry Eddy OBE (1910–23, 1936, 1939); and George Albert Holch JP, who was chairman on six occasions, made an alderman of the Harrogate District in 1974 and was chairman of the governors of King James's School from 1956 until his death in 1977. Of special interest is Lady Evelyn

Basil Thomas Woodd, of Conyngham Hall, barrister, JP and Conservative MP for Knaresborough from 1852. He was chairman of the new Urban District Council, formed in 1894.

Collins OBE, a cousin of Winston Churchill and chairman of the council in 1934–5, who in 1951 sold to the KUDC her home, Knaresborough House, where the town council still meets. Lady Evelyn's husband, Col W F Collins, was a magistrate and chairman of the bench for twenty-five years. The acquisition of Knaresborough House followed that of the other stately home, Conyngham Hall, where Harold Mackintosh of toffee fame had lived from 1924 to 1942, and which was bought by the council in 1946.

The fire brigade in about 1890 – all volunteers. Back row from left: T Hurren, J Hoy, George Wilson (captain), C Luty, T Lund and A Mason. Front: unknown little boy mascot, R Coates, Major R H Gill DSO and J Jennings. The fire engine (1774) still works and can be seen in the museum with some of these leather buckets.

Thomas Stead, the High Street butcher who was chairman of the council for thirteen successive years (1904–16).

Let us not forget the loyal service given by people not normally in the public eye. Castle Mill now had hard-working owners in the Carson family. Mary Lund worked for a time with Mr Henry Carson, then seventy-six, and she recalls how he courageously came back as managing director when his son, 'Mr Joe', collapsed and died in his early fifties. Then there was, for example, Harriet Wilson, who retired in 1930 after sixty-two years' unbroken service as a weft-winder; and such men as 'Jimmy' Fountain, Lewis Plaxton, 'Billy' Emmett (later chairman of the council) and Mr J R Wood, who ended as a director, having started at Waltons half a century earlier as office-boy. Long service in trades, crafts and shops, such as Dinsdales or Parrs, gave the community remarkable stability.

A good-humoured glance in the direction of Harrogate in this 1906 postcard linking the Knaresborough prophetess with the Old Sulphur Well.

MOTHER SHIPTON'S PROPHECY
"WATERS shall yet more wonders do, HOW strange, yet shall be true";

REGISTERED J.O

APPOINTMENT OF TOWNS BELLMAN, KNARESBRO' NOV. 21. 1907.

A competition held on the 21st November 1907 to revive the
ancient office of town crier or bellman. The bailiff, Mr Russell
Oates, holds his staff of office, while a contestant reads aloud from
a 1906 newspaper.

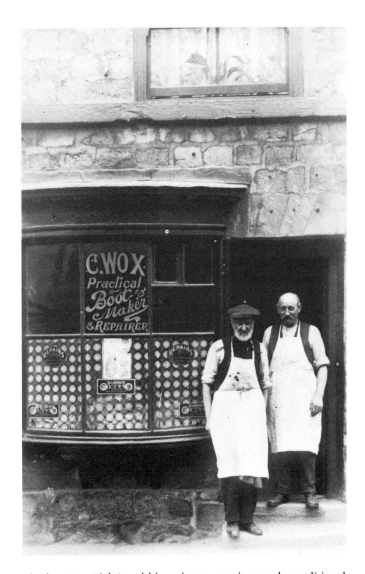

Charles Wox (right) and his assistant carrying on the traditional trade of cordwainers or shoemakers around 1900. Billy Wox, son of Charles, worked at the same High Street shop till his death in 1978.

Knaresborough's royal linen in the experienced hands of Miss Harriet Wilson at Waltons Castle Mill, where she worked for 62 years as a weft winder, retiring at the age of 75 in 1935. Her father and grandfather each served Waltons for 48 years, her sister for 33 years and her brother for 23 years.

Employees of the gasworks before the First World War. Dating
from 1824, this was one of the oldest gasworks in the country.

A historic contribution in service to the wider community was made by Philip Inman. Born in humble circumstances in a thatched cottage in Water Bag Bank in 1892, and closely connected with the nearby parish church, he started work as a paper boy for Parrs, then was a bottle-washer and errand-boy for the Oldest Chemist's Shop. Eventually he went to Charing Cross Hospital, where he served for sixty-six years as secretary, then chairman, then life-president. In 1947 he was created a peer for his service to the public (which included chairmanship of the BBC, the Tourist Board and British Rail catering), and proudly took as his title Lord Inman of Knaresborough. There had, in fact, been a Lord Knaresborough in 1906, when the title had been chosen by Sir Henry Mersey-Thompson of Kirby Hall. This caused a public outcry in Knaresborough, and the council sent him a long letter of protest, pointing out that he had no family connections with the town. In contrast, Knaresborians were delighted to be identified with the new Lord Inman.

Amongst Philip Inman's happiest memories were those of the early years of the twentieth century, when the Wednesday market was a lively place of free entertainment. As well as country folk there to sell their produce, the market was visited by an open-air dentist, a 'Corn King' and – as Joseph Fountain's painting shows – Jim Plummer, the breezy fishmonger, and Bob Morrison, who always drew a crowd to see him juggle with his crockery and chamber pots, sometimes breaking one on purpose. The most bustling time of all was in November, when the 'Status' hiring fair took place, with farm hands and girl servants being taken on for a whole year's employment. In addition to the weekly market, there were occasional visits from a circus or fair set up on the field beyond Fysche Hall.

These cheerful, carefree times were suddenly clouded over by the monstrous First World War. We can scarcely begin to imagine the untold hardship and grief experienced by the people of Knaresborough – and every other community – between 1914 and 1918, when 156 Knaresborough men were killed. Three names especially have come down to us: John Taylor, the first volunteer to enlist; Walter Malthouse, the first to be killed in action, on the 9th May 1915 when he was twenty-one, and Lieutenant D G Turnbull of the Royal Flying Corps, killed when his plane crashed into the Nidd near Chaffey Dam on the 15th April 1917. It is interesting to note that the Knaresborough Volunteers, as in previous centuries, had their own band – the ancestor of the excellent Silver Band of today – just one example of the patriotic spirit which sustained the town during those four sombre years.

After the war Knaresborough resumed its role as a picturesque market town, ideal for those who wanted to relax by the castle or down by the river. Punting was especially popular in the leisurely twenties and thirties, as we see from railway posters of the time. Thousands of day-trippers came here by train and by coach – no longer as spa visitors from Harrogate, but ordinary families from as far afield as Newcastle. There were royal visitors, too, including Queen Mary. Every sunny weekend, both banks of the river were thronged with people, many walking through the Dropping Well Estate to emerge at Low Bridge and the House in the Rock, even more crowding Waterside, with its boat-landings, Shipley's ice-cream, the Hermitage tea-gardens and the Old Manor House Cafe; and towards the end of the day, perhaps carousing in one or more of the forty-four public houses! The town was also popular with gypsies, some of whom had settled here, adding one or two Romany words to the local dialect, such as 'charver' (from charvo) meaning 'lad'.

The market in the early years of the twentieth century. The original of Mr Joseph Fountain's painting can be seen in the Mercer Art Gallery, Harrogate.

The view from the railway viaduct looking towards High Bridge seen by the thousands of visitors coming to Knaresborough by train in the 1920s or 1930s.

Punting on the river – one of the traditional delights offered to visitors by rail between the wars.

John Taylor, proudly offering himself as a volunteer – the first
Knaresborough man to enlist in the First World War. The scene is
in the crowded market place. John was one of those who came
back.

The war memorial before the top was blown down and replaced by
the present stubbier version in the early 1930s. To the right is the
Sebastopol cannon, presented to the town in 1857.

Knaresborough Volunteers of the National Reserve with their
band, ready to leave for active service, August 1914.

Knaresborough soldiers, having completed training in Scarborough, waiting for the train that will take them on their way to the battlefields in 1914. To the right of the lamp is the vicar, Canon W E Hancock.

Disciplinarian headmaster, Mr H J Tyack-Bake, with staff and pupils of King James's Grammar School. This photograph was taken soon after the school moved to the site off York Road, where it was opened by Lord Harewood in 1901.

'Gaffer' Joe Smith with some of his lads at Castle Boys' School in about 1920.
Back row from left: Billy Todd, C Norton, Joseph Fountain, R Weston, H Dix, (?) White, F Colley, 'Lol' Horsman.
Second row: Jackie Smith, F Eshelby. G Mudd, B Newby, (?) Harrison, R Harper, (?) Morrel, F Richardson.
Third row: M Flynn, G Calvert, T Ledgeway, H Shaw, H Stoker, R Sorrel, 'Nobby' Thompson, P Clapham.
Fourth row: A Birch, G Wood, G Campbell, Headmaster, B Mason, A Newbould, S Peake. Front: B Airton, 'Boy' Plummer.

The last boat to be built in Knaresborough (about 1927) in the
Sturdy boatyard. From the left, Frank Sturdy, George Smith (who
worked as ferry-man and boat-builder here from 1913 until 1939)
and George Smith senior.

By 1931, Knaresborough was still a compact little
town of character, with a population of only 5,942.
Housing increased very gradually, its first council
house being built in 1920 in Stockwell Avenue, and a
further 250 completed by 1939. One of the most
important aspects of the council's work was slum
clearance. So many of the quaint streets which made
the town so appealing to visitors consisted of sub-
standard housing, externally old-world charm but
internally squalid. Though a safe supply of water was
now piped from Harrogate, and the smelly old privies
(1,760 tons of 'night-soil' shifted in 1902!) had been
replaced by water-closets, and gaslight by electricity,
insanitary and overcrowded houses abounded. We see
this from the reports of the medical officer to the
council, Dr I D Mackay, who recorded as houses
'totally unfit for habitation', 113 in 1924, 143 in 1928
and 131 in 1930. By the following year, demolition had

Lady Evelyn Collins OBE, JP, opening Fysche Hall playing field
on the 2nd September 1929, with Councillor R Holmes and the
first children to make official use of it.

reduced this to six. In our more conservationist times, many of these would have been saved.

Compared with the substantial edifices of the Victorian period, such as the town hall (1862) in the market place and the banks in High Street, there was not much public building in the first half of the twentieth century. Exceptions were Park Grove Methodist Church, Scriven (1904), the council offices in York Place (1910), the sanatorium – later general hospital – at Scotton Banks (1937) and King James's Grammar School, opened on a new site off York Road by Lord Harewood in 1901. In spite of the valiant work of the hard-caning headmaster, H J Tyack-Bake, the school closed down for a while, but eventually became one of the most highly-reputed grammar schools in Yorkshire under A S ('Sam') Robinson, headmaster from 1922 to 1950. He increased the number of pupils from 126 to around 450, and in 1933 the school expanded into additional classrooms and laboratories.

A significant contribution to history was made by a boy who entered the first form of the grammar school in 1927. Though he was not Knaresborough-born, and travelled here each day from Wetherby, the town can be proud of having educated James Harry Lacey, who in the Second World War became famous as the ace fighter-pilot 'Ginger' Lacey. During a total of 87 air combats he shot down 23 enemy planes, mainly during the Battle of Britain, more than any other RAF pilot. No wonder he was awarded the Croix de Guerre and the Distinguished Flying Medal with Bar, as well as eight other medals.

Less spectacular, but of equal importance, was the war effort made by the people of the town, who adopted HMS *Wallflower*, raised a record amount of War Savings, manufactured parachutes, wove government cloth at Waltons, and saw Scriven Hall and Park requisitioned by the army. The names of the fifty-four service personnel killed in the Second World War can be seen on a plaque in the parish church and on the war memorial in the castle grounds. Few towns can have a memorial in a setting as moving as this – appropriately military, yet surrounded by beautiful scenery and with the peaceful sound of the river below – an atmosphere appreciated each Remembrance Day when the town gathers here to honour those killed in war, the first wreaths being laid by the mayor and the British Legion.

James Harry ('Ginger') Lacey, winner of the Croix de Guerre, Distinguished Flying Medal with Bar, and famed pilot of the Battle of Britain, who was educated at King James's Grammar School.

Veterans of the Second World War at one of the town's annual
Remembrance Day services: Jack Brier (left) and Walter Whorley.

Mr A S ('Sam') Robinson, headmaster of King James's Grammar
School from 1922 to 1950.

Lord Inman of Knaresborough being presented with an
illuminated address by Councillor J Lingard JP, to mark his
elevation to the peerage, on the 19th April 1947.

Lord Inman greeting an old friend, Mrs Smart. To the right is Lady
Inman and Councillor Albert Holch.

Lord Inman accepting the freedom of Knaresborough with Army and RAF cadets, Scouts and boys from Castle School in attendance.

The official opening of Knaresborough House as offices of the
Knaresborough Council on the 12th May 1951. Councillor
Bertram Ackroyd addresses the councillors, their wives and
representatives. In front of Lady Evelyn Collins is the key of this,
her former home.

The hub of the town – Knaresborough's unusual market cross. The old cross of 1709 was replaced by a gas-lamp, then an electric one. The date on this cross by monumental mason Cecil Naden is mcmliii (1953).

Postwar changes were slow to appear, but when they came they were radical. First was the complete reorganisation of education in the town. King James's Grammar School, under its dedicated headmaster, Mr Frank Brewin, had extensions made in 1964, including a new school hall, and in 1966 celebrated its 250th anniversary. For this occasion Mr Brewin made a point of registering a new coat of arms for the school (unlike the council emblem, which is simply a design based on a seventeenth-century seal). Five years later, however, the grammar school ceased to exist as a separate entity, and became incorporated into the new King James's School, an 11-18 comprehensive, opened on the same site in 1971 – and officially opened the following February by the Duchess of Kent.

At the same time the County Secondary School vacated its buildings in Stockwell Road. These were taken over by Castle Junior School, with the result that all the town's primary pupils now had good accommodation. Along with his small army of teachers, Mr Brewin worked hard to establish a harmonious, well-organised school – with 1,850 pupils at its peak. Alas, in 1975, just when he was beginning to see the fruits of his labours, he collapsed at his desk and died shortly afterwards – six weeks before he was due to retire. He was followed by Mr John Moreton, and in 1981 by Mr John Forster. Founder's day, introduced by Mr Brewin in 1956, is still observed each October by King James's School, which gratefully remembers Dr Chaloner and James I, whose Stuart tartans have formed part of the attractive school uniform since 1971.

Hot on the heels of comprehensive reorganisation came the change in local government. In 1974, Knaresborough lost its ancient independence and became part of the Harrogate District, its affairs now controlled by the Harrogate Borough Council. The Town Mayor of Knaresborough still wears the chain of office of the former Chairman of the KUDC and

HRH the Duchess of Kent with Mr Frank Brewin, headmaster, at
the official opening of King James's School.

presides over the fourteen elected members of the town council, but this now acts mainly in an advisory capacity, and its will has often been frustrated by the higher authority, beset by financial problems. Even so, through the council the requirements of the town can be made known in the corridors of power, and, though there is always the feeling that Knaresborough should have a bigger share of the District cake, the town has benefited from such developments as the Old Courthouse Museum (1977), the Holch Memorial Garden (1980), the warden accommodation of Collins Court (1984) and Hewitson Court (1986) and after many years of campaigning a swimming pool (1990).

The majority of development, however, has been private. In addition to a number of light-industry firms in the town, mainly on the estate on Manse Lane, and long-established firms such as Kitchings and Pickles Ointments, speculative landowners and builders have spread their ever-expanding housing estates over the green fields to the east and south. This has created a vast suburbia of dormitory and retirement homes out of all proportion to the small historic heart of the town, and helped to increase the population from 8,590 in 1950 to more than 14,000 in 1990. This means that there is the prospect of Knaresborough becoming far less cohesive than in the past, with fewer of its residents identifying themselves with the town and its traditional character.

Yet the sense of community can still be seen in Knaresborough's hundred or so societies and organisations, some of which have a long history – the cricket club, for example, having been founded as far back as 1815. There are also well-attended annual occasions – usually with the Silver Band in support – such as the carol service in the market place, the Edwardian Fair, the Boxing Day tug-of-war, Remembrance Day, the King James's Fun Run, Children's Day – and the Bed Race, organised since

The coat of arms of King James's School, incorporating symbols of the Honour and Forest of Knaresborough, as well as of James I. The school motto, in Latin, is from Psalm 116: 'What shall I render unto the Lord?'

King James's School tartans – Royal Stuart (red), Hunting Stuart (green) and Dress Stuart (beige).

1966 by the Round Table, and typical of the town's vigorous response to charitable needs. To this must be added one of the most successful town-twinnings in the country. Since 1969, Knaresborough has been linked with the German town of Bebra, with many hundreds of ordinary people – not merely civic leaders – making exchanges and Anglo-German friendships, especially the young people of King James's School and the Brüder-Grimm Schule in Bebra.

Tourists come here from many other countries, and from all over the kingdom. Though commercial interests seek ways of attracting even more visitors, and though Knaresborough, like other towns of a similar size, certainly has its economic problems, any fine day will draw the crowds here, especially at weekends and on market days, when they are greeted by the town crier, an ancient office revived by the Chamber of Trade in 1988.

'Oyez! Oyez!' The town crier, an ancient office revived in 1988, admirably filled by the colourful enthusiast Sid Bradley.

Castle Girls' School (1961), winners of the prize of 'complete suits of clothing' (right) awarded annually since the bequest by Charles Marshall in 1823, and the Stevens Bibles given in memory of Maria Stevens (died 1840) of St John's Church. From left: Heather Brearley, Carol Milner, Ann Kaminski, Susan Welch.

Most of the visitors come here because they are delighted with Knaresborough's incomparable blend of the historic and the picturesque. I am sure they would want us to keep it this way, conserving for future generations the wonderfully individual character of our heritage.

The town-twinning ceremony in Bebra (June 1969), the start of a flourishing partnership. Councillor Albert Holch with the Bürgermeister, Herr A-W Mende, next to whom is the Town Clerk of Knaresborough, George Barnett.

Blending the new with the old – Gracious Street Methodist Church, built in 1975 on the site of the Victorian chapel of 1868, with the Holch Memorial Garden to the right.

The River Nidd near the site of Knaresborough Priory.

BIBLIOGRAPHY

Atkinson, W A. *Knaresborough and its Manor Houses* (1924).

Calvert, Michael. *History of Knaresborough* (1844).

Grainge, William. *Knaresbrough* (1865).

Hargrove, Ely. *History of Knaresborough* (first edition, 1775).

Inman, Philip. *No Going Back* (1952).

Jennings, Bernard (ed). *A History of Harrogate and Knaresborough* (1970).

Kellett, Arnold. *The Queen's Church* (1978).

Kellett, Arnold. *Knaresborough in Old Picture Postcards* (1984).

Kellett, Arnold. *Exploring Knaresborough* (1985).

Kellett, Arnold. *King John in Knaresborough* (Yorkshire Archeological Journal, 1990).

Kellett, Arnold. *Companion to St John's* (1990).

Kellett, Arnold. *The Knaresborough Story* (1991).

Kershaw, Mary. *Knaresborough Castle* (1987).

Knaresborough Civic Society. *Knaresborough Conservation Area Buildings* (1973–6).

Watts, R F, and Hunt, M. *King James's Grammar School* (1966).

Wheater, William. *Knaresburgh and its Rulers* (1907).

In addition, there are several historical leaflets on Knaresborough topics by Mary Mann, published by the Harrogate Museums Service.

INDEX